Praise for

BROKEN BUT UNBOWED

"*Broken But Unbowed* takes direct aim at the constitutional imbalances that exist in our system and identifies solutions to rein in the federal government. Taking on and overcoming insurmountable challenges is not new for Greg Abbott, and his plan to restore the Constitution is bold, compelling, and worth a read."

—Newt Gingrich, former Speaker of the House

"The Constitution was created to guide and bind our country, to hold authorities to their duties and responsibilities, yet the Founders' vision is being trampled upon by a federal government and judicial system run amok. Greg Abbott's *Broken But Unbowed* provides a refreshing look at how We the People can take back our government, and return power to where the Founders intended it to be."

—Bill Bennett, #1 *New York Times* bestselling
author of *The Book of Virtues*

"My good friend Governor Greg Abbott has dedicated his career to preserving America's liberties by fighting for and defending our constitution. Like all Americans, Greg has faced difficult challenges, but it's only strengthened his resolve. If we want to take our country back, we need to listen to leaders like Greg. *Broken But Unbowed* provides a blueprint for how we can begin to fix our nation and return our country to the vision our Founding Fathers intended."

—Chuck Norris, *New York Times* bestselling
author of *Black Belt Patriotism*

"Governor Abbott is a visionary. He has overcome his personal obstacles by envisioning a life of achievement and service—which he has accomplished. He sees a stronger, safer, and more free Texas with his courageous call for a convention of the states—an idea whose time has come. Abbott embodies the courage, tenacity, and foresight of our founding fathers and the heroism of the men at the Alamo. Come and get it—*Broken But Unbowed* will inspire you to greater heights in your own life and to a greater call for action within your own state and the United States of America."

—Janine Turner, *Washington Times* columnist

BROKEN
BUT
UNBOWED

The Fight to Fix a Broken America

GOVERNOR GREG ABBOTT

**THRESHOLD
EDITIONS**

New York   London   Toronto   Sydney   New Delhi

Threshold Editions
An Imprint of Simon & Schuster, Inc.
1230 Avenue of the Americas
New York, NY 10020

First Threshold Editions paperback edition February 2017

THRESHOLD EDITIONS and colophon are
trademarks of Simon & Schuster, Inc.

For information about special discounts for bulk purchases,
please contact Simon & Schuster Special Sales at
1-866-506-1949 or business@simonandschuster.com.

The Simon & Schuster Speakers Bureau can bring authors to your live event.
For more information or to book an event, contact the Simon & Schuster Speakers
Bureau at 1-866-248-3049 or visit our website at www.simonspeakers.com.

Interior design by Renato Stanisic

Manufactured in the United States of America

10 9 8 7 6 5 4 3 2 1

Library of Congress Cataloging-in-Publication Data

Names: Abbott, Greg, author.
Title: Broken but unbowed : the fight to fix a broken America / Greg Abbott.
Description: First Threshold Editions hardcover edition. | New York:
    Threshold Editions, an imprint of Simon & Schuster, Inc., 2016.
Identifiers: LCCN 2016016561| ISBN 9781501144899 | ISBN 9781501144943 (ebook)
    | ISBN 9781501144936 (pbk.)
Subjects: LCSH: Abbott, Greg. | Governors—Texas—Biography. | Texas—
    Politics and government—1951– | Republican Party (Tex.)—Biography. |
    Abbott, Greg—Political and social views.
Classification: LCC F391.4.A23 A3 2016 | DDC 976.4/063092 [B] —dc23 LC record
available at https://lccn.loc.gov/2016016561

ISBN 978-1-5011-4489-9
ISBN 978-1-5011-4493-6 (pbk)
ISBN 978-1-5011-4494-3 (ebook)

Dedication

This book is dedicated to three women whose love and support inspired me to overcome life's challenges.

First, my mother, who instilled in me the drive and determination to never give up.

Second, my wife, Cecilia, whose unfailing devotion helped me piece my life back together. She has stood by my side for more than three decades as we've overcome challenge after challenge.

Third, my daughter, Audrey, who is a constant inspiration and compass for my life. She is a daily reminder of the joys and importance of parenting, as well as the necessity of keeping our constitutional freedoms intact for future generations.

Contents

BROKEN
BUT
UNBOWED

One Second

Our lives are not defined by our challenges, but
by how we respond to those challenges.
—GOVERNOR GREG ABBOTT

I've been known to get a bit emotional during graduation ceremonies.

The feelings of past accomplishment and future hope are rarely experienced in the same moment.

I remember my wife, Cecilia's three college graduations, celebrating the bachelor's and two master's degrees she earned. I watched her overcome so many challenges and experience so much joy on her journey to becoming a teacher, a high school principal, and the first Hispanic first lady in Texas history.

Then there's our daughter, Audrey's high school graduation. Just thinking about that day can make my eyes water—a bittersweet mixture of pride and sadness as she stepped into another season of life. She has always been a reminder of the joy that only a child can bring. The first thing I see when entering my office is a huge picture of our daughter when she was four years old. I'm holding her in one arm and she is beaming a big, radiant smile. That picture is a daily reminder of why I go to work. I want every child to smile, to hope, to dream, and to succeed.

I've had the honor of speaking at high school and college graduation ceremonies across my state. These opportunities allow me to remind new generations that as they embark on the next chapter of their lives, they can overcome any obstacles that may come their way.

There's another reason graduations mean so much to me. The last picture of me walking was taken at my last graduation.

In May 1984, with a mix of exhaustion and excitement, I walked across the platform to receive my diploma from Vanderbilt University Law School in Nashville, Tennessee.

MOVING QUICKLY

Three years before getting my law degree from Vanderbilt, I graduated from the University of Texas with a degree in finance. A few months later, Cecilia and I were married. Instead of a honeymoon, we packed and moved into the next chapter of our lives, when I began three years of intense law school study.

In my final year at Vanderbilt, I secured a job at a prestigious law firm in downtown Houston named Butler & Binion. This position was exactly what Cecilia and I were aiming for as a young couple. The future we had dreamed of was on the brink of becoming a reality.

We packed our bags in Nashville and headed to Houston, where we found a small apartment complex that attracted many other young professionals embarking on their careers. Our new home was on

Allen Parkway, just a short drive to downtown Houston, where the offices of Butler & Binion were located in the city's second-largest skyscraper.

Since my new job didn't officially start until September, Cecilia found a job at a nearby retailer, Frost Brothers. The upscale clothing store was just seven blocks from our apartment, so she'd often drive home for lunch.

Although I graduated from law school, I had not yet taken the next step in a young lawyer's journey: the state bar exam. Fortunately, a law school classmate of mine, Fred Frost, had also moved to Houston to begin work at another large law firm. He needed a place to stay until after the bar exam, and we both needed a study partner.

Cecilia and I now had new jobs, in a new city, in a new apartment—and a new roommate!

Before newly minted law grads can become lawyers, they have to pass the bar exam. Even after years of school, and landing a job, all my professional dreams hinged on passing this three-day test, which is held only twice per year, in late July and February.

Pass the exam and you're licensed to practice law. Fail the exam and you'll have to study until next year's test. And hope you still have a job.

Because the stakes are so high, people often enroll in bar review courses; mine began in June. From the day Cecilia and I arrived in Houston, my new full-time job, if you will, was to dedicate myself to this course, and pass the bar exam.

Fred and I had classes in the evening and studied during the day. Sometimes we studied together, coaching each other, and sometimes alone. But we often took an afternoon break to exercise. I was a competitive runner in high school and kept at it through my college years. For me, running was a refreshing break from sitting at a desk.

JULY 13, 1984

Although Butler & Binion was a relatively large law firm, it wasn't stuffy. Its trademark was the firm's family-style friendliness, from junior staff all the way to the managing partner. The firm hosted entertaining events during the summer to woo law students who would become the next class of lawyers for the firm. The big event each summer was a formal dinner at the Houston Country Club. Tuxedos, gowns, music, and dancing were all a part of this traditional summer dinner.

For a couple of twenty-somethings fresh out of college, this was quite a splashy affair, and definitely not what we were accustomed to. We were concerned about paying the rent, settling into a new city, waiting for health insurance to begin, and all the other challenges young couples have when they start their professional lives.

We were grown-ups, but this formal event made us feel like kids.

I remember dancing with Cecilia, smiling and marveling at how wonderfully this new chapter of life was unfolding. It seemed we'd stumbled onto a movie set—a film with a jubilant ending.

This was the beginning of the life we'd been striving for, and a tangible step toward the vision we shared.

It was a magical night.

JULY 14, 1984

The next morning, I kissed my wife goodbye as she went off to work. Even though it was Saturday, I went to work, too, at my desk—the same one I used throughout my entire law school career.

On my desk, beside the stacks of books and papers, were airline tickets we'd purchased for a trip to London.

Traveling to London—or some other overseas location—after the bar exam was a tradition in some circles. New law grads often take a month off after the July bar exam, since results aren't received until November and it may be the last opportunity to take that much time off until their careers are concluded, far in the future.

With my job beginning in September, the timing was perfect. After years of grueling study, Cecilia and I were also looking forward to this trip as the honeymoon we never had. Our wedding was just two weeks before I began law school. We spent our "honeymoon" packing and moving and readying for the rigors of law school.

London would be a vacation—and honeymoon—worth the wait.

And if that wasn't enough, in two weeks, after completing the bar exam, I'd be free from tests forever. Or so I thought.

READY TO RUN

That afternoon, after several hours of study, I shifted my focus from the thick law books to the treasured plane tickets, smiled, and shouted to Fred, "Let's go jogging!"

This interruption was no shock to Fred, who was studying in his room. We often took a running break.

A few minutes later, we were out running on well-kept sidewalks that sliced through manicured lawns of an upscale neighborhood, west of downtown Houston.

From my days in Little League baseball to high school football, and an undefeated regular season in track, I had always loved to run. The challenge of running, and the physical exertion, always gave me a renewed vigor.

Whether it was athletics, mowing lawns in the summer, or hauling steel in a forge factory, I'd always felt a physical, mental, and emotional renewal from hard work. Believe me, running in the July heat in Houston was hard work.

It was a typical muggy afternoon, but windy and overcast. Fred and I headed down the sidewalk at a brisk pace. The burden of my studies began to fall off my shoulders with every stride.

We usually ran side by side, trading good-natured verbal jabs along the way. But whenever the route wasn't wide enough, I found myself sprinting ahead. About ten minutes into our run, I noticed the sidewalk ahead was about to narrow. I moved in front of Fred.

ONE SECOND

The first shock was the sound—a loud explosion that sounded like a bomb had exploded about ten feet away.

Reflexively, I turned my head to the right, where the sound originated. It was a tree. A big oak, well over fifty feet tall, with a trunk two or three feet wide—and an enormous crack at the base.

And the tree was falling exactly where I was running.

Think of the sense of panic you feel when you perceive imminent danger. That sudden sinking feeling in your stomach when your heart abruptly stops, then races rapidly. That moment of fright that makes your hair stand on end. Then multiply it times a hundred. That's what I felt.

In a nanosecond, thoughts raced through my head.

If I stop or keep going straight, I'm gonna get clobbered, and I can't go left because cars are parked there. Go right!

The next thing I knew, I was down. Flat on my back. The entire catastrophe—from the time I heard the sound until I hit the ground—lasted no more than a second.

The good news was that I was still conscious. The bad news was that I had not lost consciousness. The pain was immediate, excruciating, and unrelenting. I had broken bones in the past and had a concussion playing football. But this was altogether different.

The pain was magnified by my inability to breathe. I'd had the wind knocked out of me before but this was beyond comparison. Trying to take in air ripped me with stabbing pains. Any attempt to exhale was sheer torture. All I could muster were short, shallow gasps.

I didn't know what had happened, but I could tell it was bad.

STAGES OF SHOCK

Everyone who suffers a serious injury goes through some instant stages. First there is the immediate shock to the body. Then, instinctively, the body and mind transition into survival mode. One second I was running. The next second, all I could think about was what I could do to survive.

Fred took a look at me and said he would run to a house and call an ambulance. These were the days before cell phones.

I was afraid to move because I had no idea what damage had been done to my body. So I just stayed motionless on the ground, faceup, waiting for what seemed like decades for the ambulance to arrive. But I had little choice. Any attempt to move punished me with even more pain.

As I waited and waited, lying flat on my back, I felt a weird sensation that my legs were frozen in midair, in the position of a runner's stride, but unable to move. It was as if rigor mortis had frozen my legs the moment the tree hit me.

Then the sickening thought struck me, that maybe I was paralyzed, with my legs stuck in the running position. Slowly, excruciatingly, without raising my head to look, I reached with my right hand to feel my legs in the air. But they weren't there—or weren't where they seemed to be.

I kept feeling for them and finally realized they were on the ground. I could feel my right leg with my hand. But my leg didn't feel my touch.

This, I realized, *must be paralysis.* My injury could be *really* bad.

At that moment, I perceived my life had forever changed. Even the tormenting pain seemed to be eclipsed by a sudden sense of doubt and uncertainty.

Once again, thoughts raced through my head. I remembered watching a movie with my wife a year earlier about a man who had been paralyzed by an accident. At the time, I told my wife that if that ever happened to me, just put me to death.

I wondered what was going to happen to me. Would I be able to walk? Would I be able to work? Would I be able to remain married? How would I be able to take care of my wife? What in the world was going to happen to my life?

When the ambulance finally arrived, the technicians assessed the situation and brought out "the board." It's the wooden board you sometimes see accident victims or injured athletes strapped to. When you see the board you know the situation is grave. I did, too.

The emergency medical team used care in slipping the board under me, but it didn't make things any less painful. When they slid the board under me it felt like it was made with shards of glass grabbing and clawing my body with each and every movement.

As I was placed in the ambulance, Fred reassured me the best he could, and said that he'd get Cecilia and bring her to the hospital.

You never really comprehend how jarring a pothole is until you're riding in an ambulance, on a board, with vertebrae splinters piercing your spinal cord.

Spinal cords are pure nerves. The feeling of a broken vertebra scratching against your spinal cord can only be described, and I apologize for the graphic illustration, as if dozens of needles were stuck into your eyes—every time we hit a pothole or turned a corner.

Greg's Not Okay, Is He?

As you can imagine, Cecilia vividly remembers every detail of that day.

While at work, she noticed an afternoon storm and heard the sound of a lightning bolt a few blocks away.

The lighting strike had knocked out power, and the store was completely dark. The manager locked the doors and wouldn't let anyone in or out.

Cecilia was quite embarrassed when the manager informed her, "Someone named Fred is here, and insists on speaking with you. He said he needs to know about Greg's insurance."

"Where's Greg?" she asked Fred as they walked outside.

"Greg went ahead to Twelve Oaks Hospital. He wasn't sure about the insurance or something like that."

Confused, Cecilia agreed to follow Fred to the hospital in our car. On the way there, she began to think something might be seriously wrong. Yes, we'd discussed health insurance the previous week, but why would Fred stop by the store?

Her fears grew as she entered the hospital and was escorted to the emergency room by Fred and two police officers.

He's gone, she thought.

"Greg's not okay, is he, Fred?" she whispered.

"I need you to be strong," he replied in a frighteningly serious tone. "Just be strong. I'm here for you."

A nurse led her to the emergency room, where I had been placed. Cecilia later recalled that moment and, despite seeing me on the hospital bed, her overwhelming emotion was joy. She was simply grateful to find me alive.

Run Over

The medical team at the Twelve Oaks emergency room used scissors to cut off my clothing and assess the damage to my body. The doctors said my back looked like it had been run over by a car. There was even a black and blue stripe across my back, the width of a car tire.

They pelted Fred, Cecilia, and me with questions about what had happened, in their efforts to plan treatment.

My breathing was getting even more torturous and labored, so communicating with Cecilia and the medical staff was difficult. I was incapable of completing sentences and could only gasp a word at a time.

I was in such severe pain that the staff couldn't communicate with me very well, either. Cecilia wasn't getting information, presumably because they were trying to protect her. In fact, she didn't fully understand the accident until she read about it in the newspaper the following morning.

The scene was chaotic.

Even worse, the pain was increasing by the minute. It had gone beyond the initial shock to a penetrating pain that felt like a tidal wave had begun to overcome me and pull me away from the shore. It became a struggle just to hang on to consciousness—and life.

I expected some type of emergency procedure. I anticipated that any minute I would be whisked into surgery, or at least have X-rays. I needed to know what was wrong, and I needed relief. Stat.

But the doctors remained uncertain how to respond. They gave me some oral painkillers while they huddled, and while I waited. For hours.

Finally, a doctor came into the room and announced, "We can't do anything for you here. We need to move you."

Houston is home to one of the world's largest medical centers, the Texas Medical Center, which includes the highly acclaimed Hermann Hospital, which has a Level I trauma center and resources for major surgeries and spinal care. It is located just two miles from my accident site.

For reasons that are still a mystery to me, the ambulance team had taken me to Twelve Oaks Hospital instead of Hermann Hospital. It turned out that my injuries were beyond the capabilities of what Twelve Oaks could treat. Twelve Oaks offered basic care but not the level of treatment I needed.

Hours of precious time had been lost.

The Twelve Oaks emergency team loaded me back on the dreaded board for another jarring ambulance ride, this time to Hermann Hospital, a mile away.

SURVIVE

There comes a time when the body is encapsulated in so much pain a person simply doesn't care anymore. All you do is survive. I had reached that point.

It was now about four hours after the accident. This whole time, I had several vertebrae in my lower back crushed into fragments and splintered into my spinal cord. Several ribs were broken and vital organs were damaged. Internal bleeding had begun.

The Hermann Hospital emergency medical team immediately hustled me into an ER surgical room.

This was 1984—prehistoric compared to today's medical technology and knowledge. They didn't have MRIs or other advanced devices available to see the extent of the internal damage in my back and abdomen.

Barely alert, I was told that they needed to determine the extent of internal bleeding and where it was coming from—and they had no time to waste. They needed to immediately perform a diagnostic peritoneal lavage, a surgical procedure to determine if there was any blood in my abdomen.

The medical staff didn't know if I had ten minutes or ten hours left. They just needed to move fast. Their focus was solely on saving my life, not reducing my pain or establishing my comfort.

I lay on a cold metal table in a chilled room filled with bright lights and a swift-moving medical team. A nurse came up and gently cupped my head into her hands as the team hurriedly plugged lines of blood and other fluids into different parts of my body.

The nurse holding my head patted it and softly said, "Just turn your head, and let it out." She knew I was about to vomit as an involuntary reaction. The surgeon then began slicing my skin below my navel at the same time they were beginning anesthesia.

Finally, thankfully, I simply passed out.

The next thing I remember was waking up in the intensive care unit, where I stayed for about ten days. I hoped the most difficult times were behind me. It turned out that the pain and the physical challenges were just beginning.

Again, medicine at the time was not as advanced as it is now. I had to wait for several days, with bone fragments lodged in my spinal cord, because the surgeons could not operate until the swelling went down in my torso.

The pain was incomprehensible. And hence I lay virtually motionless in the hospital bed, living from one morphine shot to the next.

Life was distilled down to a fundamental focus: I simply needed to survive physically.

There were times in the ICU when I didn't know if I was going to survive. I was now living minute to minute. On one hand my dire circumstances were overwhelming. On the other hand, my life was surprisingly clear—everything outside my hospital room had no relevance whatsoever. All that mattered was that I survive another minute, one more minute.

INTENSIVE

If I had the same accident today, I probably would have been out of the hospital and into a physical rehabilitation center in ten days. For me, in 1984, this hospital was my home for the next month and a half.

I had plenty of time to think when the morphine allowed. And I had a new vocabulary word to ponder: *paralysis*.

A neurosurgeon came to see Cecilia and me during my stay in the hospital. He was very nice but very frank.

"You'll never walk again, Greg."

I was extremely upset, not only about the diagnosis, but also because of the clarity of the verdict.

"Are you sure there's nothing that can be done?" I pleaded.

"Yes. I'm sure," was the answer, every time.

REALITY CHECK

There was certainly a grieving process. I experienced every thought and emotion you can imagine, and many you can't imagine.

As the days and weeks wore on, and I was transferred to rehab, the grieving process unfolded. My focus became, "Okay, here's the situation, this is what we need to do."

One day, Cecilia asked me how I felt. I suppose she asked me this question a thousand times, but on that day I replied, "I feel relieved."

Sounds like a strange thing to say, doesn't it? But on some level, I felt like I had been to hell and back. And I was still alive. There is an ironic liberation that comes with that experience.

These were some of my more upbeat thoughts.

The other reality for me was this: a life once filled with confidence was now suddenly riddled with self-doubt.

I was the baseball player who knew, with absolute certainty, that if I could get on first base, there was no way the pitcher and catcher could stop me from getting to second base. I was the student who knew, through sheer hard work, I could pave a pathway to success.

But that person was a fuzzy memory. At twenty-six years old, he was in a body cast, facing an uncertain future.

I suddenly faced obstacles that made it more challenging, if not impossible, to achieve my goals. Not only that, but the prospect of doing simple, daily tasks seemed daunting.

There were questions of all sizes bombarding my tired mind. How would I take care of myself? How would Cecilia cope? Could we have the child we dreamed about? Could I take care of my family financially? Could I even work?

INSURANCE

Worries came and went. Small victories were celebrated.

After several surgeries and a prolonged stay in the hospital, I went to The Institute for Research and Rehabilitation. In the process of rehab at TIRR, I regained full use of my hands and arms. I found physical therapy to be just the challenge I needed. Finally, an opportunity to work out again!

After about six weeks at TIRR, I was able to go home for a few months and begin the process of learning to live in a wheelchair. Cecilia and I were surprised to find the management of our apartment complex had converted our apartment and entryway, making it accessible by wheelchair.

We were worried about our health insurance coverage but soon discovered we had some coverage through a policy we'd purchased the previous year in Nashville. This wouldn't cover all the costs, but every bit helped—financially and emotionally.

After learning about the accident, many people came to our aid with food, visits, prayers, and encouragement. They included my new colleagues at Butler & Binion.

For those whose interaction with the legal community has been, let's say, less than positive, you might think lawyers are a heartless bunch. They could have been thinking, *If the new hire has a broken back and can't come work, we have to find someone else for the position.*

Cecilia tells me that one of the first full sentences I was able to put together when I was in the ICU was a request. "Please call the law firm . . . and tell them . . . I might need a later starting date."

Little did I know that the attorneys, who shared in that magical evening at the Houston County Club the night before my accident, were the people who had taken off work to find the best doctors for me. Even more, they were like family to Cecilia, helping her navigate not only my care, but everything she needed as a new resident of Houston. The waiting room was always full of family and our new friends from the law firm.

I was one of about thirty-five new lawyers for the firm, so they could've done without me. But their lead lawyers and partners took time off to be at the hospital.

While I was still in the hospital, the law firm put me on the payroll, even though they were probably as uncertain as I was about my ability to work again.

Unchanged

This period of time is difficult to describe.

In one sense, my world was forever changed in an instant. But I came to realize that I hadn't changed. And, I began to think, my dreams didn't have to change either.

Before my accident, I had rarely been in contact with people with spinal cord injuries. But now, on a daily basis, I was interacting with others who experienced them, too. We were all paralyzed in one fashion or another. A primary concern of many if not most of those who faced this sudden shock was the goal of finding a way to walk again. They were going to devote their lives to being able to walk. I commend that attitude, which has led to countless medical advances, but I had other battles to fight.

I was broken, externally, but not in my heart and mind. My legs were now wheels. The doctors told me that even if I could move my legs, I still could never walk. That was my reality in 1984. I had a choice. I could fight against that reality or I could begin devoting all my energy toward the future.

To the surprise of many of my friends, I had no desire to seek experimental treatments that might restore movement or feeling in my legs. Instead, I decided to accept my circumstance and do as much as possible with it.

I can't fully explain this mindset.

Part of this resolve might be the drive instilled in me from my youth by my parents. Part may be my God-given nature of being goal-oriented, hopeful, and practical. And part of the equation is certainly the grace of God—on me, and through Cecilia, family, friends, and so many wonderful medical professionals.

UNBOWED

I've gotten pretty good at popping wheelies, negotiating obstacles, and overcoming challenges in my wheelchair. It's second nature now, just like a person walking up steps without thinking about all the intricate motions involved.

Cecilia and I laugh about it now, but at the time, during one of my first returns to life in our apartment, I gave her quite a scare.

One Sunday afternoon, while watching a Dallas Cowboys football game on TV in the living room, I got a little excited. I've always been a pretty expressive fan. One particular play had me so riled up that I threw popcorn at the TV. And I fell out of the wheelchair.

It's a good thing I was still wearing my body cast.

When Cecilia came home, she gasped. I was quite a sight, I suppose, lying on the floor in front of the television, surrounded by a lot of popcorn. A normal occurrence in a new circumstance.

Life was going to be different, but I didn't have to change. Life was going to be good.

Somehow.

Two

The War of Independence

I believe there are more instances of the abridgment of the
freedom of the people by gradual and silent encroachments of
those in power than by violent and sudden usurpations.
—JAMES MADISON, SPEECH AT THE VIRGINIA CONVENTION, 1788

With each passing day in the intensive care unit, it became increasingly difficult for the nurses to find a spot on my buttocks to insert another morphine shot. It resembled an overused pincushion.

I remember the discomfort of cottonmouth even more vividly. I wasn't allowed—let alone physically able—to drink any fluids or consume anything by mouth. No moisture crossed my mouth and my saliva production was sapped by the side effects of the drugs I was given. My mouth became drier than a West Texas dirt road in the middle of summer.

The one comfort I craved was for my wife to dampen a washcloth with water and a little lemon juice, and hold the cloth to my mouth. I was incapable of moving, or doing anything for myself. My entire existence, for many days, was reduced to the mere desire to temporarily relieve my cottonmouth.

When you cling to life, looking forward to a lemon-moistened cloth as the highlight of your day, you gain a new perspective on the troubles we all face in life.

Once the swelling in my back went down, the doctors were able to perform what was called a myelogram. This is a medical test to find any problems associated with the spinal canal. The myelogram involved the insertion of dye and a series of X-rays to determine the damage to my spinal cord.

That's the *theory* of the test from the doctor's perspective.

For me, it was altogether different. The insertion of the dye, and the X-rays that followed, required moving my body multiple times into different positions, including turning me onto my stomach for the first time since the accident. With the vertebrae fragments still penetrating my spinal cord, each movement felt like the doctors were beating me with a prickly cactus.

Only after this test were the surgeons able to locate and remove the bone fragments in my spine.

During surgery, the doctors fused my broken vertebrae together and inserted Harrington rods along my spine. These stainless steel rods, designed to stabilize the spine, remain in my back to this day. I'm still amazed how surgeons could put a piece of medical equipment into your back in 1984, and more than thirty years later those rods are still doing their job, without any complications.

TILTED

After ten days in ICU, back surgery, and three weeks recovering from surgery, I was getting quite accustomed to being on my back. Sure, to prevent bedsores, the nurses would help me move onto my side for a few hours at a time, but generally, I was horizontal 24/7 for weeks. The head of the bed couldn't even be raised. It was essential to keep my back flat and immobilized to promote healing of my battered spinal cord, and to strengthen my newly fused vertebrae.

One day, a special day, at about ten o'clock in the morning, the room was filled with light. Six hospital staffers came in and announced I was going to be placed on a tilt table. I would temporarily move out of my bed for the first time in weeks. It was a sign of progress, but it was also a terrifying prospect.

A tilt table is like a bed—a bed with heavy straps. I was placed on a board, painstakingly moved to the tilt table, and strapped in.

My equilibrium had been reset to the horizontal level. The tilt table was going to give my equilibrium a rude reminder about the forces of gravity.

I was warned in advance that this experience typically caused nausea. It didn't make sense to me. They were only going to tilt me up a little bit. It should be no big deal, right?

The nurse told me the bed would be tilted only ten degrees up, but for a person who'd spent almost a month lying flat, the motion felt like a gyroscopic ride at Six Flags Over Texas.

After the tilting began, and I was locked into position, I had only one thing to say: "Better get a bucket."

FLASHBACKS AND DREAMS

Three months in a hospital is probably a bit like being in prison. Sure, I had visitors, but they could come and go freely. I was confined to one bed in one room.

Like others confined to cells, I had access to books and, after a few weeks, was able to read. And read. Any genre would do. I read some fiction, nonfiction, magazines, and even the fine print on the IV bags. Sometimes I read to distract my mind; other times, especially toward the end of my incarceration, I read to get back on track with the life goals Cecilia and I were clinging to.

I began to wonder about what I'd be able to do with my life after leaving the hospital. I had never contemplated being in such a situation. I traced back over my life, thinking and pondering where I had been and what I had done, and tried to piece together some pathway forward.

In elementary and middle school, participating in activities like Cub Scouts, Boy Scouts, and sports had a big impact on me. I learned the value of goals, teamwork, and achievement.

Cecilia reminded me—and ribbed me—about a tale from when I was in first grade at Pinewood Park Elementary School in Longview, Texas. Every year around Christmas, each classroom would vote for the king and queen of the class, and in first grade, I was voted the king!

The simple voting machines would have been the envy of Broward County, Florida. Every student competing for the titles had a jar with their name on it, and voting classmates put pennies in the jar of their pick for king and queen. I ended the election cycle with the most pennies!

I still credit my mom for stuffing the ballot box. Or did she? I never knew.

The first time I formally ran for an office was in sixth grade at Judson Junior High. I ran for treasurer. A friend and I made campaign posters and placed them all over the school. I lost that race to an "establishment" eighth grader.

When I was in high school, seniors were required to take a government class. One of the exercises was to hold a mock trial. Some students got to be lawyers; others were witnesses, jurors, and judges. I played the role of a lawyer, which was one of the experiences that stimulated my interest in law.

This matched another related interest of mine in high school: history.

I was fascinated with our nation's history, and was one of the few students who "lettered" in both sports and academics. To receive an academic letter, you had to have the highest score combined from grades and a special subject test. I was the student who received the letter sweater for history. Yes, an academic letter sweater is not exactly the kind of thing a teen wears around the neighborhood. It never left my closet. Cecilia reminded me that it was *still* in the closet.

Most college kids go through the exploratory process of finding out what interests them. They move away from home for the first time and try to figure out who they are. I was no different.

The first major I signed up for in college was political science/pre-law, but after two years on that track, my practical side took over. I moved into a major that offered multiple career pathways—business. I graduated from the University of Texas with a finance degree.

It turned out that my initial instincts were right, and I returned to the law pathway I had initially embarked on.

In law school, just as in college, different students choose different pathways. Some students focus on business law, others on international or health care law. Many focus on litigation. For me, law school was about one predominant topic: the Constitution. I devoured this document.

The Constitution merged my interest in law and history. It captured the majesty and genius of our nation's founders and it laid the foundation for all other laws in our country.

It was in law school that I first realized that not every judge followed the rule of law. In fact, by my observation, there had been many disturbing departures from the rule of law, contrary to what had been enshrined into our foundational document. It was then that I first began thinking if I ever had the chance, I would do something to restore the rule of law.

While lying in that hospital bed, I doubted if I would ever have anything to do with the Constitution or history. But that didn't abate my interest.

One of the books I read in the hospital was a compilation of texts and speeches that are significant to United States history. Included in the book was the Declaration of Independence. I read it, and reread it, absorbing the notion that people have the power to declare their own independence. *That concept* was exactly what I needed.

QUINTESSENTIAL AMERICAN

A quintessential American embraces the concept of rugged individualism, self-sufficiency, and optimism.

Growing up mowing lawns as a teenager, and working hard outdoors, I had a sense of security—knowing I could accomplish anything I put my body and mind to. In one second on that hot July day in 1984, I experienced crushing insecurity.

The accident put me in a position of dependence, which is not a position I like, or was accustomed to.

Independence is part of the American DNA. That's why our

country began with the Declaration of Independence, as opposed to the Declaration of Dependence. Our nation was formed by people who were trying to get away from the control imposed by a distant government. We were born as a nation in search of one thing: freedom to chart our own pathway.

My time in the hospital definitely gave me time to ponder independence and dependence, insecurity and security. On one hand, I experienced greater insecurity. All my expectations and plans had vaporized in one second. On the other hand, I experienced support from my wife that defied description. One important characteristic to understand with Cecilia is that she is strongest when she is offering support.

Whether it be caring for a fellow human being, or a little injured puppy, she excels at tending to those in need. One example is how for over ten years, she's delivered Meals on Wheels and built wonderful relationships with the people she serves. It's just the way she is.

Cecilia was strong and supportive from the day we married in 1981 to the moment I write this, and she has never wavered. I can assure you that's a testament to her character, not my charm.

If you want to know the meaning of love, look no further than my wife, who stood by my side during the most painful period of our lives. It's easy to recite the marriage vow, *For better, for worse, in sickness and in health.* It's awe-inspiring to see someone embrace that vow.

ROLE MODEL

In October 1984 I was discharged from TIRR Rehabilitation Center—earlier than expected. But it wasn't good news. My stepfather passed away and TIRR allowed me to leave two days before my scheduled release to attend the funeral with Cecilia and my mother. My biological father died in 1974, and my mom remarried a few years later.

I attended my stepfather's funeral wearing a body jacket, a form of cast called a turtle shell. Turtle shells are rigid on the outside but soft on the inside, and custom-made to fit from below the belt line to the armpits. They're designed to keep the torso immobilized but allow movement of the hips and arms.

I felt like a robot, but at least I could begin to gain some freedom of movement, with protection. I wore this shell until Christmas of 1984, when I was "unwrapped."

The Monday after the funeral, I reported for work at my high-falutin law firm in a ginormous building in downtown Houston, rolling around in my wheelchair. While my colleagues were in gray suits, I was in my turtle outfit and sweats.

In reality, the work I was doing at the law firm probably wasn't bringing in any revenue. But I don't think it's a stretch to say my presence brought revenue to the firm in other respects. When other lawyers arrived in the morning, I was already there. If they wanted to go home early, they'd have to walk past me—the guy in the body cast recently discharged from the hospital.

When they considered calling in sick, they pictured me wheeling myself into the office. Slow and steady wins the race, as the saying goes, for turtles and attorneys.

I figured that even if I wasn't making it rain money for the firm (I hadn't even taken the bar exam), I could still be a role model. I also wanted my work ethic to express sincere thanks to the firm, and its lawyers, for the remarkable support they provided Cecilia and me as we navigated substantial challenges.

Pearls of Independence

With a desire to show Cecilia appreciation for her amazing love-in-action, I hatched a plan to sneak out of the apartment and buy her a special Christmas gift.

She was still working at Frost Brothers and was scheduled for extra hours to help with the holiday shoppers. This gave me some free time to go to a store undetected.

Since I was unable to drive, I called a taxi to pick me up and take me to a jewelry store. It's hard to comprehend what it's like to get in and out of a car without the use of your legs, in a body cast.

The taxi driver was surprised but seemed up for the challenge.

I told him the destination and asked if he could wait in the car while I completed the purchase. This information, along with my physical condition, opened up a friendly conversation. I answered his questions about the accident, my wife, and the modest gift I had in mind.

He helped me out of the car, into my wheelchair, and opened the door of the store. Much to my surprise, he also followed me into the jewelry store.

I asked the salesperson for a pearl necklace, in the price range I could afford, and we were shown a simple but elegant choice. I say *we* because the cabdriver and I were now in this together.

The driver reached out and picked up the necklace and, like a master jeweler, carefully inspected the piece with his oil-stained hands before handing it to me. If that wasn't enough, I now had an advocate in price negotiation.

"No, no, no," he protested. "That is too much for this necklace."

I was no expert in pearl buying, but I wasn't expecting to haggle with a salesperson at a reputable jeweler.

"Thank you very much," I said. "But the price is fine."

Although I was embarrassed by my new friend's desire to help me, the man's unconventional candor and helpfulness were refreshing. It was part of my new normal.

During the taxi ride home, I realized how symbolic this experience was. I was no longer in charge of my own life.

I was now dependent on others for the most basic of tasks, which I'd always taken for granted. But since I am a person deeply connected to independence, that adventure made me look forward even more to what was coming next.

In January 1985 I went back to TIRR for what you might call "graduate school" of physical rehabilitation. During this time I learned more about gaining independence, including skills like opening doors, crossing streets, and my favorite: learning to drive a car using hand controls.

Our group would head out into the streets of Houston, in our wheelchairs, and learn to navigate our new world.

As with my trip to the jewelry store, I experienced a mix of feelings, dealing with new realities of life without the use of my legs, and making progress in my fight to regain some independence.

FALLING OVER THE BAR

By July 1985, I was ready to take the three-day bar exam. It's a high-pressure test for most people, and I was no different.

Cecilia drove me to the Houston Convention Center, where the exam was being held, parked the car, and wrangled the heavy wheelchair out of the trunk. I maneuvered into the chair and was on my way to the testing room with fifteen minutes to spare before the exam began.

Cecilia helped me navigate a curb—this was in the days before the Americans with Disabilities Act. She "popped me up" over the curb. This involved me doing a wheelie while she held the back of the chair to make sure I didn't fall over backward.

Midway through our maneuver, we experienced what seemed like one of those slow-motion scenes in a movie. We heard a sharp "click" as a wheel fell off, and a thud, as I fell out of the chair onto the hot street.

With only ten minutes until exam time, I finally lost it.

The healthiest person in the world would feel enormous stress about taking a bar exam. But as someone learning to live life in a wheelchair, as a paraplegic, in a new job, and after a year of painful rehab and endless study, the frustration boiled over.

Cecilia later told me this was the first time she saw something in me . . . panic. Vulnerable fear.

After being thrown onto the asphalt, wondering how to fix the wheelchair and get to the exam on time, I simply couldn't take it anymore.

Thankfully, people walking nearby rushed to help. They were able to get the tire back on the chair and helped us inside. I was reminded once again why I appreciate the Texas spirit—a special, and big, part of the American spirit. The assistance I received was just what I needed to regroup and focus.

I made it into the exam room with two minutes to spare. No sweat.

The bar exam has so many questions it is virtually impossible to answer them all. There is an odd liberation that can come from the certainty that you don't know the answer to a question. One of the fill-in-the-blank questions asked: "What is a writ of capias?" I didn't have a clue. I could leave it blank and move on. Or I could have some fun. I wrote: "A type of fish."

I still don't know if I got any points for that answer or not. A few months later, however, I learned that I had more than enough points to pass the bar exam.

Thanks to my wife, the wonderful physical rehabilitation specialists, my colleagues at Butler & Binion, and the grace of God, I was now licensed to practice law.

This was another big step toward my independence. I was ready to roll.

Three

Unity of Faith

We may then unite in most humbly offering our prayers and
supplications to the great Lord and Ruler of Nations, and beseech
Him to pardon our national and other transgressions; . . . to render
our National Government a blessing to all the people by constantly
being a Government of wise, just, and constitutional laws . . .

—PRESIDENT GEORGE WASHINGTON, IN HIS OCTOBER 1789

PROCLAMATION OF AN OFFICIAL THANKSGIVING HOLIDAY,

SHORTLY AFTER THE CONSTITUTION WAS RATIFIED

As the grandson of a pastor, my life was infused with faith from the very beginning. Cecilia and I share the belief that God loves each of us, and has a purpose for all of us. We believe in the miracle of life, the miracle of marriage, and the miracle of meeting each other.

In 1978, Cecilia applied and was accepted to two universities: the University of Texas and what is now called Texas State University. Her dream was to follow in the footsteps of her parents and become a teacher. Texas State was one of the premier colleges for educators in the state. She chose it.

That August, Cecilia and her mom left their home in San Antonio and headed north on Interstate 35 to San Marcos, where Texas State is located. En route, Cecilia suddenly had the overwhelming impression not to attend Texas State, and an unexplainable desire to attend the University of Texas in Austin.

She announced this unexpected revelation to her mother, who was understandably skeptical and caught completely off guard. Cecilia's dorm at Texas State was already selected and her classes scheduled. She pleaded with her mom to just drive an additional thirty minutes north to Austin to see if there was still an open position for her at the University of Texas.

"Please, please, Mom! Let's just go and check it out."

They first went to the registrar's office to see if her acceptance would still be honored. It would.

But then the admissions secretary informed them, "You're not going to find a place to live. All the dorms are full—it's going to be impossible." And it *was* impossible.

Cecilia and her mom drove all around the UT campus, and indeed the dorms were all filled. They visited off-campus dorms and came across The Castilian. As they walked up to the front door, Cecilia immediately felt this was the place for her.

The young man at the front desk was pleasant and sympathetic. But his response was the same as at all the others: the dorm was full. Not only were all the rooms reserved, but there was also a long waiting list.

Cecilia sat down on a nearby bench, overwhelmed with emotion. It had been an unusual and exhausting day. The disappointment and confusion surrounding her unplanned adventure were hitting home.

As her mom tried to comfort her, the man from the front desk walked up to them and announced, "You're not going to believe this, but we just got a cancellation. I'm going to go ahead and slip you into a room."

That room "just happened" to be in the same dorm I recently checked into. The next day, Cecilia and I met. We soon became friends, and discovered we had so much in common—including the same birthday. The dorm held a big birthday party for us. Cecilia turned nineteen, and I turned twenty-one. Our mutual bonding was just beginning.

In 1981, three years after we met, we were married—thanks to divine intervention, and Cecilia's leap of faith from one university to the other. I don't pretend to understand the reason why everything happens. I simply believe that purpose can be found in all that happens.

I've always felt a deep and abiding connection with God. I've never known what He had planned. But I did know it was my duty to try my best to follow Him.

Our marriage was more than the joining of two families. It was a uniting of cultures—my Anglo heritage and Cecilia's Irish and Hispanic heritage. We may have come from different backgrounds, but we shared the same foundation of faith.

Sounds like America, doesn't it?

UNUSUAL PERSPECTIVE

From the first day of our marriage until the day I passed the bar exam, Cecilia had been the primary provider for our family. It was now time for me to go to work, and for Cecilia to return to school—where she earned three degrees and became the teacher and principal she longed to be.

Although I'd always been a hard worker, I suppose the fact that I began my law career in a wheelchair made me extra diligent. Everything from getting to the office to retrieving files just took more time. Besides that, I wanted to prove to the partners in the firm, and my peers, that they'd made the right decision in hiring and supporting me.

There were many specialty divisions at our firm: corporate securities, real estate, oil and gas, wills and trusts, etc. I chose litigation because I thought it was the best path to address the constitutional conundrums I had learned about in law school.

Problem One: Big-city law firms typically don't have much constitutional litigation.

Problem Two: All young lawyers, even those in wheelchairs, start at the bottom rung and have to work their way up. I began by reviewing documents, researching cases for more senior lawyers, and preparing all kinds of pretrial motions for judges to consider.

Monday mornings brought what's called the "motion docket" at the courthouse. In this area of law, most of what attorneys do is file motions. They file a motion for summary judgment, a motion for discovery, a motion for more motions, and so on.

A motion is a plea to the court, asking the court to act on certain pretrial matters. When you think of "motion," think of "move"—as in, *move the case along.*

On motion docket day, the courtroom is filled with lawyers crowded onto benches. On one particular Monday, I arrived at a room so full, there was nowhere to park myself but next to the jury box, which was already crammed with other attorneys.

At nine o'clock the noisy courtroom was interrupted by the customary loud call from the bailiff, "All rise!" And they did—everyone except me.

The judge entered the room, walked to the bench, and prepared to take his seat. As he scanned the courtroom his eyes fell on me. Because I was on the side of the jury box away from him, he could see I was sitting, but could not see why.

"Sir, when the bailiff says 'all rise,' it means stand up," the judge said curtly as he remained standing. The courtroom went from quiet to deafeningly silent.

I grabbed the wheels on my chair and rolled toward the bench. "Your honor, I would if I could," I said with a sideways grin.

The judge was incredibly embarrassed, of course. I'm pretty sure everyone, including the judge, laughed. What I know for sure is I never lost another motion in that court!

Not long after that, I was asked to be the lawyer who would present the case to a jury—flying solo. It was a simple case, representing the Houston Metropolitan Transit Authority, a/k/a the bus company. A bus had rear-ended a car. The driver and passenger of the car claimed they had whiplash. I was told to just keep the damages awarded by the jury as low as possible.

"What?!" was the incredulous response by the partner I reported to when he learned of the verdict. The jury agreed with my arguments that the driver of the car that was rear-ended was the one at fault. The bus company—never a sympathetic party in front of a jury—didn't have to pay a dime.

I simply used common sense to defend my client. I explained to the jury the reality of driving in downtown Houston: "You can't just unexpectedly slam on your brakes without considering what's behind you." It's a basic driving school lesson that the car driver neglected: always look in your rearview mirror before slamming your brakes.

Good start for a rookie.

It was during those early years in my career that I realized a few unique advantages of practicing law in a wheelchair. When I approached the jury, I was at eye level with them, not looking down on them. I was one of them, not lording over them. It was easier to connect.

My wheelchair played a leading role in my next trial. I represented a hospital that was sued by a man who claimed injury in a "slip and fall" incident.

His allegations seemed dubious, as he walked around the courtroom with a cane, claiming he couldn't work or function because of his "debilitating" injury.

In my cross-examination, I pulled up right next to the jury and asked, "So you're telling this jury that because of this slip, your use of a cane means you can't go get a job? You can't do work of any kind?"

The irony of his claim, that he couldn't work while using a cane, became obvious. Suddenly the man was enraged. He ran toward me and started beating my wheelchair with his cane, apparently forgetting that he needed to use it!

Another win. I was on my way.

NAVIGATING THE SYSTEM

I went on to represent a wide variety of clients, from individuals to big international businesses. But the clients that meant the most to me were the hospitals and nurses that I represented.

One case still stands out to me. I had the honor of representing a group of nurses who felt their lives had been ripped apart when they were sued. We won.

I had never forgotten the way a nurse gently held my head while

I lay helpless on that emergency room table, and how nurses pieced my life back together when I was hospitalized. I was proud to help them navigate the legal system as effectively as they had helped me navigate the health care system.

I gained a sense of fulfillment by using the law to help my clients. But I grew frustrated about how the system was working.

Too many times in the courtroom, I could tell that judges had not even examined the briefs that I'd spent countless hours—and thousands of my clients' dollars—meticulously researching and writing. Even worse, I found that some judges simply wouldn't apply the law as it was written, and instead based their decisions on other factors, including their personal feelings.

I knew there had to be a better way. It was the same frustration I felt when reading court decisions during law school that seemed to stray from the law. But now there was something I could do about it.

In Texas, we elect judges at all levels of the state judicial system. In 1991 an incumbent trial court judge in Harris County (in which Houston is located) announced he wasn't running for reelection. I announced I was running for that seat. After a hotly contested race, in 1992, at the age of thirty-four, I became one of the youngest lawyers to be elected as a judge in Texas history.

True to my commitment, if a lawyer had an argument to make, I listened. When a motion was filed, I read it. Where a law applied, I applied it. My diligence earned me the highest ranking among judges in the Houston Bar Association evaluation.

My efforts also got the attention of the newly elected governor of Texas—George W. Bush. In 1995 he appointed me to an open seat on Texas's highest court, the Texas Supreme Court. I was just thirty-seven at the time of the appointment. I would become one of the youngest justices to serve on the Texas Supreme Court.

I'll remain eternally grateful to our forty-third president for the trust he placed in me.

It was a major change of position for me within the legal system. No longer was I the lawyer—or law student—simply reading court opinions. As a trial court judge I had presided over jury trials and ruled on motions. I had to read countless higher-court opinions, but didn't write opinions myself. Now I was the *author* of those opinions. My goal was more than just deciding cases correctly. I could now demonstrate to the legal world—and the world at large—that the rule of law was followed and applied. It was an attempt to correct the erroneous pathway of judicial activism that had deviated from the rule of law intended by the Founders.

And I finally got to grapple with the constitutional issues I craved. Some involved the U.S. Constitution; many more involved the state constitution. Either way, the underlying principle was the same: to show that strict application of the law was the proper approach.

When I was on the Texas Supreme Court, cases were assigned to justices by way of a drawing. Case names were typed on blue cards and placed upside down on the conference room table. The justice who picked up a blue card with a case name on it was given the first crack to draft the opinion in that case. If the opinion draft won the support of a majority of the court, it was the decisive opinion.

By luck of the draw, or providence, I happened to be responsible for a large share of constitutional decisions during my tenure on the court.

And because I wanted to share my approach of constitutional interpretation with the next generation of lawyers, I taught a constitutional law course at the University of Texas School of Law.

But after a while, something became obvious. I was looking through a rearview mirror.

The cases we were deciding involved facts that were sometimes five or ten years old. Except for emergencies, a lawsuit typically isn't filed until a year or two after an event occurs. Then it takes another year or two for the case to get beyond the trial court, then another year or two to get beyond the court of appeals, and another year or two for the state supreme court to decide.

LOOKING FORWARD

Yes, we were the highest court in the state, and in that regard the final word about the law in Texas (except in criminal cases that went to the Texas Court of Criminal Appeals). But, again, our focus was on applying law to what happened years ago.

I wanted to look forward, and apply the law to new challenges that were coming our way, rather than enforcing law on what had been. When John Cornyn, the Texas attorney general at the time, announced in 2001 that he would be running for the United States Senate, I knew this was the opportunity for me to look at the horizon, and see where I could take the law.

I immediately announced I was going to run for attorney general and handily won an otherwise hard-fought race.

I embarked on a bold agenda:

- Create a new Cyber Crimes Unit to arrest child pornographers and child predators who were using the Internet to prey on children.
- Create a new Fugitive Unit to track down and arrest previously convicted sex offenders who violated their parole. I wanted to get to them before they got to their next victim.

- Use new tools to prosecute identity thieves who were wreaking havoc on seniors.
- Expand Medicaid prosecutions to recover taxpayer money fraudulently bilked from the Medicaid system.
- Deploy Peace Officers from my office to partner with the Texas Department of Public Safety to crack down on cross-border money laundering and drug and human trafficking.
- Prosecute election fraud.
- Elevate the Texas child support system—that recovers money for children—to be ranked number one in the U.S.

My team and I accomplished all that and more during a time when I became the longest-serving attorney general in Texas history.

Whenever you see someone who has achieved some level of success, you often find they have been surrounded by extraordinary people. Whatever success I've had is due in large measure to the people around me, whether it was my supportive parents or a guiding Scoutmaster, an inspiring coach or teacher, caring doctors and nurses, encouraging colleagues, my remarkable staff, or my loving wife.

When I was elected attorney general, I knew more than ever that we had to assemble a staff that could support the bold initiatives I wanted to achieve.

One of those initiatives was to continue the process of steering our legal system back onto a path that applied the principles enshrined in the Constitution. I needed to do more than respond to legal actions. I needed to initiate action.

To do that would require the help of a rare talent. Someone who was not only a master of the Constitution, but could also wield it to protect the liberty we inherited. Someone who could do more than represent the state in courts of law, but could lead nationwide coalitions to help restore the rule of law. I found that person in Ted Cruz.

I appointed Ted to be solicitor general of Texas. In that role he helped lead national efforts to safeguard Second Amendment rights, to protect religious liberties, and to reassert the Tenth Amendment. And Ted was the advance guard for the very type of constitutional contest I had been seeking since law school.

Including one of biblical proportions.

Ten Commandments

An atheist was walking across the Texas Capitol grounds, saw a historic monument that included the Ten Commandments, and was offended.

No, this isn't a setup line for a joke. It was the first volley in a battle royal about the limits of government-sponsored religious expression under the First Amendment.

He filed a lawsuit challenging the constitutionality of Texas's display of the monument, insisting it should be removed.

I was even more adamant that the Ten Commandments would not be torn down on my watch. So we fought back. Texas won at the trial court and, with Ted Cruz taking the lead, we won at the federal Court of Appeals, too.

The case then went to the United States Supreme Court in 2005.

As his counsel, the offended atheist brought in one of the foremost constitutional scholars in the United States at the time, Erwin Chemerinsky. He was a law professor at Duke University and his name adorns the constitutional law book that many law students read at the time.

SUPREME COURT CASE

When the U.S. Supreme Court took jurisdiction of the case, I took over the argument. This was the challenge I had been waiting for.

Although I had served as a justice on the Supreme Court of Texas, this was my first argument to the United States Supreme Court. Few litigators ever argue before those nine justices. It was a rare and daunting challenge.

You learn something about yourself when you realize that a fight over principles means more than a fight over money. Regardless of which party won or lost, no one was going to have to pay anybody anything. But there was far more at stake in this case than with any other I had been involved in.

It seemed that through my entire adult life courts had been trying to erase God from the public square in the United States. Court orders forced prayer out of schools and mandated the removal of religious displays.

Courts repeatedly coerced believers to acquiesce to the antagonistic legal antics of atheists. The Freedom From Religion Foundation had grown in strength and was repeatedly, and rapidly, launching legal missiles at defenseless rural counties that simply wanted to display a nativity scene in the county square, as they had for decades.

It seemed that courts had gone beyond the constitutional charge against the *establishment* of religion. They were now siding with those who were hostile to religion. Courts now seemed to mandate antireligion. I felt we were on the brink of becoming One Nation Against God.

Trial by Fire

I immersed myself in legal research that Ted and his team had amassed. I honed my points through countless mock arguments before brutal inquisitors.

It's called "moot court." It's like a runner preparing for a race by wearing weights during practice, or a baseball player using a weight donut on his bat for some practice swings before stepping up to the plate. Moot court is intended to prepare the lawyer for the scorching that will take place in the heat of the argument when real judges ask tough questions.

Hopefully, without causing too much psychological damage to the attorney.

In one of my final practice sessions in Washington, D.C., a few days before the real thing, I faced a "murderers' row," a group of lawyers with more than one hundred Supreme Court arguments under their collective belts. They included the top lawyer for the United States, the solicitor general under President Bush, Paul Clement; former U.S. attorney general Ed Meese; and Jay Sekulow, one of the preeminent First Amendment scholars in America.

They were too good. They knew the justices' positions well and they knew all the soft spots in my argument. They inflicted doubt and uncertainty.

But I took solace knowing that I had one go-to argument I could rely on. In our brief,[1] we cited many places where the Ten Commandments are displayed in numerous state capitols, federal buildings, and even in the United States Supreme Court building itself. In fact, as you enter the Supreme Court courtroom, the two huge oak doors have the Ten Commandments depicted on the lower portion of each door. Additionally, the courtroom itself is decorated with a frieze of various historical "lawgivers," one of whom is Moses holding the Ten Commandments.

I hoped the irony would not be lost on the justices.

But hope is not a strategy, so I prepared notes that I could quickly glance at during the argument if needed.

They included topics from our brief like:

- The Court has consistently upheld the constitutionality of recognizing the role of religion in American culture and society. For example, the Court has acknowledged that its own proceedings open with the cry, "God save the United States and this Honorable Court." *Marsh v. Chambers*.
- In *Lynch v. Donnelly*, the Court noted that our history is filled with official references to "Divine guidance," including officially recognized Thanksgiving and Christmas holidays . . . House and Senate chaplains . . . the national motto "In God We Trust" . . . the Pledge of Allegiance.
- Justice Sandra Day O'Connor wrote in *Lynch* that the history and ubiquity of official references to God are not understood as conveying government approval of particular religious beliefs.
- The Court has deemed acceptable expressly religious acknowledgments like President Roosevelt's 1944 Proclamation of Thanksgiving, quoted at length by the Court in *Lynch*. It said: "To the end that we may bear more earnest witness to our gratitude to Almighty God, I suggest a nation-wide reading of the Holy Bible during the period from Thanksgiving Day to Christmas."

Then, I buckled my chinstrap.

The Supreme Court argument[2] was on March 2, 2005. Ironically, that date is Texas Independence Day—the day Texas declared its independence from Mexico, eventually winning its freedom. I was fortified by the Texas founders' determination to fight for independence. I would continue that legacy by fighting for our independence to continue to recognize the principles and values on which our state and nation were based.

THE BEST-LAID PLANS

For an attorney in a wheelchair, the United States Supreme Court courtroom presented a unique challenge. Lawyers argue from a podium, located between two small counsel tables. Because of the podium's height, I wouldn't be able to access it with my notes and make an oral argument from that position. So, unlike my opposing counsel, Chemerinsky, I made my presentation from the counsel table.

An oral argument before the Supreme Court is amazingly fast-paced. I'd been warned by Ted Cruz, who had clerked for Chief Justice William Rehnquist and had argued at the Court several times, that if it was structured appropriately I would be able to give an opening statement of approximately thirty seconds before being bombarded with questions by the justices.

I'd have time to say, "The lower-court decision should be affirmed for three reasons" and then quickly list the reasons before facing relentless questions from the justices.

That's exactly what happened. I had about one minute for my opening, and after that, it was continuous, rapid-fire Q&A from the justices.

The vote I needed the most was from Justice O'Connor. In the years before the Ten Commandments case, there had been multiple cases involving other religious displays, including crèches, menorahs, and crosses. Justice O'Connor was the pivotal author in most of those decisions. She is credited with revising the standard that courts use to determine if a religious display is constitutional.

Because of this, my game plan and preparation were geared toward winning her vote, knowing that if I did that, we would win the case. The answer to every question I would receive from other justices would focus on Justice O'Connor.

To win O'Connor's vote, my argument explained there was no overt religious purpose behind the Ten Commandments monument. Instead, a philanthropic group gave the monument to the state of Texas, and the state decided to place it on the Capitol grounds. I argued that the Capitol grounds was a vast outdoor museum commemorating events that had an influence on shaping the history and traditions of Texas.

I contended that the laws that came forth from the Ten Commandments had an impact on Texas history, much as they influenced the history of the United States Supreme Court, as evidenced by the various depictions of the Ten Commandments in the U.S. Supreme Court building.

Justice Antonin Scalia wasn't buying it. He suggested that if that was my reasoning, he couldn't support me.

I was undeterred. If any justice was going to uphold the Ten Commandments it was going to be Justice Scalia. I remained focused on winning O'Connor's vote.

Other justices peppered me with legal questions, hypothetical questions, religious questions, and philosophical questions. Justice Stephen Breyer asked some detailed questions concerning where in the record information could be found about what Texas had disclosed in brochures about walking tours to view monuments on the Texas Capitol grounds.

I quickly summoned a detailed answer:

"Your Honor, Justice Breyer, if I could refer you to page 205 of the Joint Appendix, it provides a description of each of the monuments on the walking tour [on the Texas Capitol Grounds]. And if I could also refer the Court to page 117 of the Joint Appendix, it shows the actual walking tour where a person would go along the process of seeing the monuments."

He gave a reassuring nod, seeming to signal not only gratitude for the information, but confidence that I had mastered my argument.

Finally, the questioning ended, and the argument was over. Chief Justice Rehnquist was absent from the argument because of illness, but he still voted on the decision. That left the senior justice—John Paul Stevens—in charge of running the courtroom proceedings that day.

To my astonishment, Justice Stevens looked at me and said, "General Abbott, I want to thank you for your argument and also for demonstrating that it's not necessary to stand at the lectern in order to do a fine job."[3]

I thanked him. Cruz, who was sitting at the counsel table with me, leaned in: "Something like that has never happened before."

ARGUMENTS AND OUTCOMES

Immediately following my oral argument, the Supreme Court heard another case[4] about Ten Commandment displays. Two Kentucky counties had posted copies of the Ten Commandments in their courthouses. The counties adopted resolutions meant to show that the Commandments are Kentucky's "precedent legal code." The Kentucky Ten Commandment displays included other historical documents containing religious references such as the Declaration of Independence and the lyrics of "The Star Spangled Banner." The displays contained information explaining the historical and legal significance of the documents and their influence on Western legal thought.

I paused to briefly listen to the argument, then hurriedly made my way to the waiting press to share my thoughts about the oral argument.

After several months, the decision was released.

I quickly looked to see who won. Texas!

Then I saw the vote count: 5–4.

All our strategy and planning had paid off, I thought. The votes broke down along the lines we assumed, and I must have picked up Justice O'Connor's vote.

Hold on. O'Connor voted against us? How could she do that? She would have to depart from her prior opinions to rule against us.

Then I wondered, *If we didn't get O'Connor's vote, how did we win? Holy cow! We got Justice Breyer's vote.*

In case you're wondering, Justice Stevens's vote didn't follow his kind comment about my argument. He voted against the constitutionality of the monument.

The opinion upholding the constitutionality of the Ten Commandments display on the Texas Capitol grounds was written by Chief Justice Rehnquist and was joined by Justices Scalia, Anthony Kennedy, and Clarence Thomas. Justice Breyer agreed with the result, but filed his own opinion.

The victory quickly turned bittersweet. In fact, it got very confusing.

Kentucky lost their case 5—4. They lost the vote of both Justices O'Connor and Breyer.

Amazing. A Court that openly displays the Ten Commandments on its doors and on its walls, a Court that just ruled that Texas can display the Ten Commandments on its Capitol grounds, also ruled on the same day that Kentucky cannot display the Ten Commandments in its courthouses.

What in the world does the First Amendment mean?

I guess it means whatever swing votes on the Supreme Court decide it means, rather than being grounded in principles established by the First Amendment's authors.

Then I understood why people were losing faith.

Four

I Think We Can

When those who are governed do too little, those who
govern can—and often will—do too much.
—RONALD REAGAN

I've read many books during my childhood, college career, and physical rehabilitation. Of all the books I've read, one of the most impactful was a short book, with pictures, read to me by my mother.

When I was about three years old, living in Wichita Falls, Texas, I went through a season of saying "I can't." Whenever my mother asked me to do something, my response was the same.

"Go make your bed."

"I can't."

"Tie your shoes."

"I can't."

Thankfully, my mother was a firm disciplinarian, and she made it very clear to me that "I can't" was never acceptable.

A memorable part of her guidance was the nightly reading of a book you've probably read, *The Little Engine That Could*. The phrase "I think I can, I think I can" still echoes in my mind.

Those words became as intuitive in my life as the blinking of an eye.

Could I overcome my paralyzing injury and build a path forward? *I think I can, I think I can.*

Could a guy in a wheelchair ever be elected to office? *I think I can, I think I can.*

My staff knows that when it comes to solving our citizens' problems, *can't* is not an option.

That means using every tool possible to ensure that the laws of this land are going to be followed—even if it requires challenging the federal government itself.

I THINK WE CAN

The very day President Barack Obama signed Obamacare into law, March 23, 2010, Texas and twelve other states took him to court. That lawsuit took twists and turns and eventually ended in a way no one expected.

This wasn't my first rodeo, as they say in Texas. I had already waged more than a dozen legal battles against both the Bush and Obama administrations.

This was altogether different. This truly was like *The Little Engine That Could* chugging up the mountain, with everyone watching from below insisting there was no way the engine would make it over.

But it was important—even essential—to climb that mountain for two reasons. First, Obamacare threatened the premier health care system in the world. Second, Obamacare posed an even bigger danger: it threatened the very liberty on which this nation was founded.

I wish the federal government would seize operational control of our border the way they've wrested control of the doctor-patient relationship.

In reality, the federal government is a complete failure at securing our border *and* at running health care. The failures of Obamacare and the scandalous neglect by the Department of Veterans Affairs (VA) in forcing veterans to wait in line for health care—and sometimes die while waiting—make one thing clear: the federal government doesn't have a clue how to run health care.

I've heard a great many stories that, sadly, prove this point.

A woman preparing to give birth, or a patient preparing for life-saving surgery, does not need the added stress of losing her trusted doctor because of Obamacare.

Seniors have been excluded from the best hospitals, and families have been stuck with hefty bills because Obamacare didn't live up to its promise.

Access to quality health care is increasingly at risk. I've heard countless doctors say they are leaving the practice of medicine because of Obamacare—leaving behind not only their profession but leaving our neighborhoods with a dwindling supply of physicians.

I suppose this goes without saying, but I'm as pro–health care as they come, and forever indebted to the incredible advances in medicine this country has produced. And that's the whole point. I'm passionately against any law or policy that reduces the quality, and quantity, of health care available to Americans.

Was our health care system flawless before Obamacare? Of course not. Were there improvements that could be made to health care without hijacking one-sixth of our economy and squeezing it into a one-size-fits-all program? Absolutely!

YOUR HEALTH AND YOUR HEALTH CARE

Just put yourself in the position of typical employees who worked for a company before Obamacare. If they lost their jobs, did they lose their auto insurance? *No.* If they lost their jobs, did they lose their homeowners' insurance? *No.* If they lost their jobs, did they lose their life insurance? The answer is *no.*

But, if they lost their jobs, did they lose their health insurance? For many, the answer was *yes.*

We should change that answer and make health insurance as portable as auto insurance.

Free-market competition has always been an important factor in improving products, services, and prices. Health care should benefit from the same economic dynamics.

We should allow small businesses and individuals to pool together for greater buying power in the insurance market. We should allow health insurance to be sold across state lines to bolster competition and give people more options—especially in the mobile society we live in today. We should expand Health Savings Accounts and put people—as opposed to government—in control of more of their money, and in control of their health care choices.

Perhaps most important, we need to get bureaucrats out of the system and allow doctors and patients to decide what's best for their health.

We need to look no further than the VA to see the future under Obamacare. Here a single-payer system has destroyed care for our nation's heroes. No veteran who has fought for this country should suffer the indignity of having their care denied due to bureaucratic bungling. It is time to renew this nation's commitment to our warriors. Having served on the front line, they should go to the front of the line for treatment.

There are many simple approaches to restructure health care and make the system more effective, and reconnect the doctor-patient relationship in ways that don't trample our constitutional rights.

The so-called Affordable Care Act and its dubious path through Congress are perfect examples of broken government at work.

This was a train wreck about to happen. I knew something needed to be done to stop it. I knew *can't* wasn't an option.

But we needed to start by stopping.

Votes for Sale

As James Madison said in 1788, it's the gradual and silent encroachments of government that are often the most dangerous. Sometimes those acts build to a crescendo until they burst into a triggering event.

In 2009, a few other state attorneys general and I saw the challenges that were being posed by Obamacare and wanted to do something about the law. We pondered our options, but none seemed promising.

The "Affordable Care Act" was a law that most people in America did not want, but it would affect one-sixth of our economy, dramatically interfere with the doctor-patient relationship, and cause health insurance premiums to skyrocket, among other consequences.

We knew the legislation would be an economic disaster. But for President Obama, it was pure political genius because he was able to pass a law that would be phased in, so the dire effects would not go into effect until he was leaving office.

Both the American people and members of Congress could see the flaws in the proposed law. Despite Democratic control of both the U.S. House and Senate, Senate Majority Leader Harry Reid remained one vote short from having the sixty votes needed in the Senate to avoid a filibuster, which would prevent the law from passing. As 2009 was coming to an end, there was an impasse.

A congressional impasse is often a triggering event for what is euphemistically called a congressional "concession." Some call it a congressional bribe.

To gain the late December vote of Nebraska senator Ben Nelson, it was widely reported that a deal was made to give Nebraska millions of dollars in Medicaid concessions. Senator Nelson then became the sixtieth—and filibuster-proof—vote on the Senate version of Obamacare. The deal was quickly dubbed the *Cornhusker Kickback*.

If this agreement had been done in the private sector, participants could have been threatened with jail. But because it was done in Congress, people simply rolled their eyes and accepted it.

This kind of behavior exemplifies both what is wrong with the way government works today, and how our government has gotten so far from what the Founders intended.

For me and my fellow state attorneys general, however, this was the spark that moved us into action.

STANDING UP

Twelve colleagues and I immediately drafted a letter, which you can see in the appendix of this book. But here are some high points of the letter:

The current iteration of the bill contains a provision that affords special treatment to the state of Nebraska under the federal Medicaid program. We believe this provision is constitutionally flawed.

It has been reported that Nebraska Senator Ben Nelson's vote, for H.R. 3590, was secured only after striking a deal that the federal government would bear the cost of newly eligible Nebraska Medicaid enrollees. In marked contrast all other states would not be similarly treated, and instead would be required to allocate substantial sums, potentially totaling billions of dollars, to accommodate H.R. 3590's new Medicaid mandates. In addition to violating the most basic and universally held notions of what is fair and just, we also believe this provision of H.R. 3590 is inconsistent with protections afforded by the United States Constitution against arbitrary legislation.

Our letter—coupled with a heavy dose of public ridicule—brought an end to the Cornhusker Kickback. But the wheeling and dealing was just beginning.

Harry Reid needed every Democrat senator's vote. Uncommitted senators were in a position of power, and they sank to the occasion. This is how *Politico* described the dubious process:

Other senators lined up for deals as Majority Leader Harry Reid corralled the last few votes for a health reform package.

Nelson's might be the most blatant—a deal carved out for a single state, a permanent exemption from the state share of Medicaid expansion for Nebraska, meaning federal taxpayers have to kick in an additional $45 million in the first decade.

But another Democratic holdout, Sen. Bernie Sanders

(I-Vt.), took credit for $10 billion in new funding for community health centers, while denying it was a "sweetheart deal." He was clearly more enthusiastic about a bill he said he couldn't support just three days ago.

Nelson and Sen. Carl Levin (D-Mich.) carved out an exemption for non-profit insurers in their states from a hefty excise tax. Similar insurers in the other 48 states will pay the tax.

Vermont and Massachusetts were given additional Medicaid funding, another plus for Sanders and Sen. Patrick Leahy (D-Vt.) Three states—Pennsylvania, New York and Florida—all won protections for their Medicare Advantage beneficiaries at a time when the program is facing cuts nationwide.

All of this came on top of a $300 million increase for Medicaid in Louisiana, designed to win the vote of Democratic Sen. Mary Landrieu.

Under pressure from the White House to get a deal done by Christmas, Reid was unapologetic. He argued that, by definition, legislating means deal making and defended the special treatment for Nelson's home state of Nebraska. "You'll find a number of states that are treated differently than other states. That's what legislating is all about. It's compromise," he said.[1]

None of these corrupt practices were proven illegal, but most Americans could smell the stench.

BUYING POWER

After sending the Cornhusker Kickback letter, our state attorneys general group expanded its efforts. We looked inside the Obamacare train that was barreling down the track toward becoming law.

What we found was far more frightening than dubious deal making. As we studied our legal research and dug into the thousands of pages of proposed law, we couldn't believe what we found. We didn't think *others* would believe what we found.

But the lawlessness was as plain as day. The Obamacare law was a direct assault on the Constitution and on liberty as we knew it. The proposed law contorted the Constitution beyond where it had ever been stretched. If we didn't stop this law in its tracks, there would be no way to ever check the power of Congress. The country would irreversibly careen down a course that threatened the principles that hold our nation together.

Our argument was straightforward: Congress can't just make up any law it wants. An act of Congress must be rooted in a legislative power given to Congress under the Constitution. That's what Article I, Section 1 of the Constitution commands.

Congress claimed that the Obamacare law was grounded in the Commerce Clause, found in Article I, Section 8. The relevant part of that section is short and simple. It gives Congress the power to "regulate Commerce with foreign Nations, and among the several States, and with Indian tribes."

Obamacare didn't involve foreign nations or Indian tribes. Nor did the lynchpin of Obamacare deal with commerce among the several states.

The lynchpin of Obamacare was the individual mandate. As even

President Obama's lawyers conceded, the Obamacare law would not work without the individual mandate.

The individual mandate is the part of the Obamacare law that forces most adult Americans to buy insurance whether they want to or not. We live in a free country, right? Not if government can force you to buy things—that's what communistic countries and dictators do.

The Commerce Clause had been stretched and stretched until it allowed Congress to regulate almost every conceivable activity. But never in U.S. history before Obamacare had Congress used the clause to compel Americans to buy a product.

If you choose to buy or sell something, Congress and the courts have decided such activity typically falls within their expanded definition of the Commerce Clause. But never had either of those branches of government dared to intrude on your freedom by forcing you to buy something.

Now Congress and the president had crossed that line. They were doing more than running government. They were dictating your life decisions.

There had to be a way to stop this. But how?

Working with the legislative branch wasn't an option, because it was the branch that just passed the law. The executive branch was the architect and lead supporter of the law, its namesake. The judicial branch was our only possible path to redress, but even it was widely recognized as upholding virtually all federal programs under the Commerce Clause.

Our group of attorneys general realized that states and individuals were the *only* hope to fight against a two-thousand-plus-page bill that was opposed by a majority of the nation.

With the help of the National Federation of Independent Business, two individuals, and twelve other states, we made the decision: we were going to take on the daunting challenge of suing the United States of America.

To add a punctuation point, the lawsuit was filed on the day the president signed Obamacare into law.

Among the thirteen states that filed the lawsuit, we joked that we felt like the first thirteen colonies fighting for freedom against a much bigger, well-funded army. But like the colonists, we knew we were fighting for a principle larger than ourselves: the timeless principle of freedom.

And, just as the original thirteen states grew into a much larger country, the number of states that joined the lawsuit grew also. When we got to the finish line, more than half of America was suing America, for redress from America.

While many Americans rejoiced that someone—*finally*—had the backbone to fight against this outrageous encroachment on liberty, the pundits scorned the effort. A piece written by Ezra Klein in the *New Yorker* captured the prevailing attitude among the intelligentsia. He wrote that it was hard to find a law professor in the country who took our lawsuit seriously.

> "The argument about constitutionality is, if not frivolous, close to it," Sanford Levinson, a University of Texas law-school professor, told the McClatchy newspapers. Erwin Chemerinsky, the dean of the law school at the University of California at Irvine, told the *Times*, "There is no case law, post 1937, that would support an individual's right not to buy health care if the government wants to mandate it." Orin Kerr, a George Wash-

ington University professor who had clerked for Justice Anthony Kennedy, said, "There is a less than one-per-cent chance that the courts will invalidate the individual mandate."[2]

To show just how far the liberty train had left the station, consider the reaction of then–Speaker of the U.S. House Nancy Pelosi. After our lawsuit she was asked by a reporter: "Where specifically does the Constitution grant the Congress authority to enact an individual health insurance mandate?" Her answer: "Are you serious?"[3]

She either had no clue, or, she knew that what they were doing was not well grounded in the Constitution. Either way, it was not the stuff that Madison and Hamilton were made of.

That is the same Pelosi who said that Congress had to pass Obamacare to find out what was in it. These lawmakers, by and large, don't have a clue about what they are imposing on their constituents. They have deeply departed from the original constitutional system that was intended to be the premier government document in history.

SERIOUS?

Yes, we were very serious.

As my fellow attorney general Henry McMaster from Carolina said: "A legal challenge by the states appears to be the only hope of protecting the American people from this unprecedented attack on our system of government."[4]

We presented a solid case to federal district judge Roger Vinson in Florida. We asked that Obamacare be ruled unconstitutional. And we held our breath.

Eleven months after filing the lawsuit, the decision was in. I remained hopeful, but was about as stunned as most everyone else.

Judge Vinson wrote: "If Congress can penalize a passive individual for failing to engage in commerce, the enumeration of powers in the Constitution would have been in vain for it would be difficult to perceive any limitation on federal power . . . and we would have a Constitution in name only. Surely this is not what the Founding Fathers could have intended."

The judge concluded: "the individual mandate is neither within the letter nor the spirit of the Constitution."

And with that, Obamacare was stricken down . . . for now.

COURT OF APPEALS

With unrestrained smugness, the Obama administration immediately appealed to the U.S. Court of Appeals in Atlanta. We now had to present the issue to a three-judge panel, two of whom had been appointed by Democrat presidents.

We were now to the semifinals of a process more important than any game. It was a process that would determine the future course of the Constitution, as well as the existence of Obamacare.

A few months later, in August 2011, just a year and a half after the president signed Obamacare into law, we won a second and profound victory for the Constitution.

As the *Wall Street Journal* reported: "A U.S. appeals court in Atlanta handed the Obama Administration its biggest defeat to date in the battle over the health-care overhaul passed last year, ruling the law's mandate on Americans to carry health insurance was unconstitutional."[5]

My fellow attorney general Bill Schuette of Michigan captured our collective feeling when he called the ruling "a huge victory in the fight to protect the freedom of American citizens from the long arm of the federal government." [6]

SUPREME ARGUMENTS

For the first time since the day the lawsuit was filed, I noticed an attitude change in the pundits—and in the president's lawyers. Gone was their swagger and the ridicule of "those pesky states." I sensed panic and uncertainty. I think they finally realized that the future of Obamacare was at risk.

But we all knew we had one more rendezvous ahead—a date with the United States Supreme Court.

Perhaps it was because of that panic and confusion, perhaps it was that they retained a sense of arrogance about government power, perhaps it was because the Supreme Court justices actually agreed with our arguments—for whatever reason, it seemed that the Supreme Court oral arguments could not have gone worse for the president's lawyers. They took a pounding.

We took cautious solace in the righteousness of our cause.

The best way to recount the moment is to quote what I said on camera at the Supreme Court steps after one day of arguments:

I just left the Supreme Court building after we had a day of oral argument where the issue before the Court is going to be whether or not they infringe on your liberty and overreach into your lives unlike ever before.

You can tell this is history in the making for two reasons. One reason is because of the massive crowds outside of the Court, where people across the country are coming here to protest against this overreaching law.

You can also see the history in the court hearings themselves. I've argued a case before the U.S. Supreme Court defending the Ten Commandments monument. I've been here about Second Amendment cases as well as other cases that Texas has had before the High Court. Every Supreme Court argument lasts one hour.

This case is not lasting one hour or even one day. This case is lasting three days in an historic moment before the U.S. Supreme Court as we work so hard to defend you, your lives, your pocketbooks, your taxpayer dollars and your liberty.[7]

THE SUPREMES/THE TEMPLE

The oral arguments at the Supreme Court lasted through the three days of March 26–28, 2012. It wouldn't take long to learn the result. The Supreme Court was slated to announce its decision three months later, on June 28, 2012.

Most of the time, the Supreme Court issues its decisions only in written opinions. Some decisions carry such gravity the justices want to read a synopsis of the opinion from the bench—the elevated area where the justices sit.

The justices clearly knew the weight of this decision and chose to read selected portions to the public.

The courtroom was packed. The stately decorum of the majestic tribunal—ornately decorated and held high with colossal marble columns—was overrun with lawyers, media, onlookers, by anyone who could get in, stuffed into every nook and cranny.

I sat in the front row.

THE SCENE

The tension was so thick you could almost cut it with a knife. The only certainty in the courtroom was that no one was certain about the outcome.

I stole a glance to my right, where Solicitor General Donald B. Verrilli Jr. was sitting. He was the top appellate lawyer for the United States, and he seemed uneasy, frequently downing gulps of water. This moment was years in the making and this decision was about to make history.

Suddenly, the thunderous announcement that the justices were about to enter the courtroom rang out: "All rise!"

The judges walked out from behind a massive maroon curtain and took their positions on the bench. As Chief Justice John Roberts began reading the decision, I heard echoes of all the naysayers who said we didn't have a chance, and the constant reminder of *The Little Engine That Could.*

The chief justice began reading his synopsized version of the opinion, signaling that he was the author of the majority decision. His facial expressions were impossible to read.

After stating some general principles on which the decision was based, Chief Justice Roberts moved to issue number one: was Obamacare a tax? As he explained, you must pay a tax before you can challenge it in court. If, in theory, anyone can bring a lawsuit before paying their taxes, then the government wouldn't have any revenue. Hence we have the Tax Anti-Injunction Act, where only under particular circumstances can someone challenge a tax before it is paid.

For purposes of the Tax Anti-Injunction Act, the Court had to first conclude that Obamacare is not a tax in order for them to even have the authority to evaluate the merits of the case.

When the chief justice read that Obamacare was not a tax I felt enormous relief. We had cleared hurdle number one. Now we would finally have a Supreme Court decision on the core constitutional issues at stake.

Hurdle number two was the central issue on which the whole case rested: did Obamacare violate the Commerce Clause? For decades, the Commerce Clause had been misconstrued and distorted to give Congress far more power than the Founders intended. Its very relevancy was on the line.

As much as we wanted to win the case, we desperately wanted to see the Supreme Court properly apply the Commerce Clause as it was written and intended.

You could sense the entire courtroom audience lean toward the bench to hear the decision. The chief justice began: "The individual mandate does not regulate existing commercial activity. It instead compels individuals to become active in commerce by purchasing a product."

Holy cow! That sounds like our argument.

The chief justice continued:

Construing the Commerce Clause to permit Congress to regulate individuals precisely because they are doing nothing would open a new and potentially vast domain to congressional authority. Upholding the Affordable Care Act under the Commerce Clause would give Congress the same license to regulate what people do not do. The Framers gave Congress the power to regulate commerce, not to compel it. Ignoring that distinction would undermine the principle that the Federal Government is a government of limited and enumerated powers.

That was *exactly* our argument.

Then the finish: "The individual mandate thus cannot be sustained under Congress's power to 'regulate Commerce.'"

I was in as much disbelief as our opponents. For years, naysayers said we had no chance. In a moment frozen in time, they were wrong. We won on the very issue Americans had been vigorously and contentiously debating for the past few years. Can the federal government force you to buy health care? The answer was a profound NO!

But then there was issue number three: the Necessary and Proper Clause of the Constitution. Even our own lawyers agreed this would be the sword that our team would die on. This clause had been applied by courts to allow Congress to do pretty much whatever it pleased.

The chief justice read the result: "Even if the individual mandate is 'necessary' to the Affordable Care Act's other reforms, such an expansion of federal power is not a 'proper' means for making those reforms effective."

That was *our* argument.

The chief justice of the Supreme Court had worked his way through the three primary issues in the case and we had won them all. This was beyond belief.

Court decisions that had frustrated me since law school were now being mended. We were returning to the rule of law rather than the rule of man . . . or so I thought.

I quickly flipped pages in my legal pad away from the notes I was taking and began hammering out a statement to share with my team.

Victory seemingly in hand, I stopped listening to the chief justice and began writing. "History has been made. The Commerce Clause was enforced. Congress cannot make Americans buy a product against their will. Obamacare is—"

I glanced up and noticed the reaction of the crowd, instead of listening to what Chief Justice Roberts was reading. The crowd wasn't reacting like I was. What was going on?

The chief justice was saying: "The Affordable Care Act describes the shared responsibility payment as a 'penalty,' not a 'tax.'"

Right, everyone knew that. President Obama himself said that it absolutely was not a tax. If Obamacare had been a tax, there's no way it would have gotten half the votes it needed to pass. That's why Congress was so emphatic that it was a penalty rather than a tax if someone refused to buy the mandated insurance. The law "penalized" people who refused to participate.

My certainty was abruptly interrupted by Chief Justice Roberts: "Congress's choice of language—stating that individuals 'shall' obtain insurance or pay a 'penalty'—does not require reading §5000A [that's the Obamacare law] as punishing unlawful conduct. It may also be read as imposing a tax on those who go without insurance."

What? Did he just say that what Congress says about a law is not controlling?

That's exactly what he said. Justice Roberts proceeded to rule that for purposes of determining whether Obamacare was constitutional, it was a tax. This is the same chief justice who just moments ago said Obamacare was *not* a tax. I'm thinking, *Where's Alice, because we are in Wonderland.*

I carved a big X across the proposed press statement I was crafting.

What the Supreme Court just said is that Congress cannot regulate inactivity, but they can tax it. If you purchase something, Congress can regulate you. If you choose *not* to purchase something, Congress can tax you.

In other words, the Supreme Court has now proclaimed, Congress has the power to tax you for your exercising your individual freedom not to buy something.

That is a tax on liberty itself.

This was bad. Really bad.

After a few minutes of continued reading from the bench, I caught myself repeatedly circling the phrase I had earlier written: "History has been made." It certainly had.

Neither the Congress that passed the law, nor the president who signed it, believed Obamacare was a tax. But because five unelected, unaccountable judges in robes decided differently and chose to redefine it as a tax, Obamacare was upheld.

It was now clearer than ever that we had become the victim of the rule of man, rather than the rule of law.

We left the courtroom, and the immense public square outside the Supreme Court building was a madhouse. As I spoke with the media it became clear that Americans were completely baffled by what had just happened.

The experience demonstrated, as powerfully as anything I had ever seen in government, how the ruling class had completely turned away from the first three words of the Constitution: "We the

People." The ruling was another step toward a nation of dictates by potentates. The Constitution was weakened, and so was the nation it had sustained.

Unfortunately, it turned out the Supreme Court was just getting started in assuming powers delegated to Congress.

Congress's words and intent were unmistakably clear when it chose to use the word *penalty* rather than *tax* as the punishment for Americans not buying health care insurance under Obamacare. When five Americans who wear robes disagreed with Congress's word choice they rewrote the law.

Three years later, in 2015, the United States Supreme Court rewrote Obamacare once again in order to save it.

Obamacare requires states to create health care exchanges where people can shop for health insurance. If a state does not create a health care exchange, the U.S. secretary of health and human services must "establish and operate such Exchange." To seemingly encourage states to create those health care exchanges, Obamacare provided tax credits for millions of Americans who bought insurance "through an Exchange *established by the State*" (emphasis added).

One problem: More than half of the states chose not to create health care exchanges. If Congress wants to create more and bigger government programs, that's its prerogative. The states don't have to be their handmaiden in the process.

The decision by so many states not to create health care exchanges meant that a substantial number of Americans wouldn't be eligible for the Obamacare tax credit. The Supreme Court concluded that "the result was an 'economic 'death spiral' '" for Obamacare.

So, to once again save Obamacare, the Supreme Court rewrote—I should say interpreted—the phrase "Exchange *estab-*

lished by the State" to mean "Exchange *established by the State or the Federal Government.*" The high court audaciously added words to the statute written by Congress.

In his dissent, Justice Scalia famously characterized this as "interpretive jiggery-pokery." He added what many Americans could plainly see: "Under all the usual rules of interpretation, in short, the Government should lose this case. But normal rules of interpretation seem always to yield to the overriding principle of the present Court: The Affordable Care Act must be saved."

When this happens, how can people have confidence in our courts and trust in our laws?

When citizens begin to lose faith in their system of government, it leads to the erosion of the fabric of this country and puts us on a pathway toward chaos.

And America is now saddled with Obamacare.

In writing the Constitution, and advocating for it, Alexander Hamilton insisted that the judicial branch of government would be the least harmful, posing the least threat to people. In many respects, Hamilton was a wise visionary. In this regard, though, he completely missed the mark. In fact, the judiciary may have evolved into the most dangerous branch of government, especially because it is the least accountable.

BEST OF INTENTIONS

It's been said that the road to hell is paved with good intentions. Even the best of intentions produce unintended consequences.

You, me, the president, members of Congress, and justices on the Supreme Court—none of us can imagine the unintended consequences that arise when we ignore the law and the foundation of our laws—the Constitution.

I'll assume for a minute that all three branches of government have the best of intentions every time they skirt around the law. But sooner or later, we all are hurt by their good intentions.

Can we find a way to clean up the mess our elected (and unelected) officials and bureaucrats have caused? Can we stop the threat to our freedom that comes from abandoning the Constitution? Can we fix the foundation of the country?

I think we can.

Five

President or King?

When the legislative and executive powers are united in the same person, or in the same body of magistrates, there can be no liberty. . . .
—MONTESQUIEU, *THE SPIRIT OF THE LAWS*, 1748

When it comes to rewriting Obamacare, the Supreme Court is a rank amateur compared to President Obama.

The president has repeatedly altered the language and intent of Obamacare, including changing rules on out-of-pocket expenses, delaying the start of the employer mandate, giving certain people—including members of Congress and their staff—and certain companies a "waiver," and changing the way tax credits are given.

Basically, he's ignored or rewritten Obamacare when the law has proved inconvenient.[1]

While some Americans may think these unilateral changes benefit them, all Americans need to realize that such presidential fiats and administrative rewritings of laws directly threaten the rule of law established in the Constitution.

What may be good for your goose today will fry your gander tomorrow.

SIMPLE GENIUS

Everyone who knows me understands I am a doting father to my daughter, whose picture adorns the entry into my office. Throughout her school years, my top priority was spending time with her.

When she was in fifth grade, I proudly took time away from work to watch her perform a school skit that reenacted the musical cartoon "I'm Just a Bill." [2] You might remember its popular theme song from Saturday morning television as part of the *Schoolhouse Rock* series. The song explained to generations of schoolchildren that a law could go into effect only if it passed both the U.S. House and Senate and then was signed by the president.

This was the elementary school version of what the Constitution commands. Article I, Section 1 says all legislative powers are vested in Congress. This language should be part of every president's oath of office.

Article II of the Constitution concerns the president. It doesn't give power to the president or administrative agencies to make law or rewrite law. To the contrary, Article II specifically commands that the president "shall take Care that the Laws be faithfully executed." Rather than allowing the president to make law, the Constitution requires the president to ensure the laws passed by Congress are "faithfully executed."

The Founders purposefully structured the Constitution this way to deny the president the ability to become like a king who could capriciously make up laws. They knew, from the lives that had been lost in the fight for liberty, the importance of creating a Constitution that prevented lawless rulers.

Montesquieu was a French lawyer and political philosopher whose wisdom was heavily relied on by the Founders, especially

James Madison. In 1748, Montesquieu explained that allowing a president the ability to make laws as well as execute them poses a threat to liberty itself:

> When the legislative and executive powers are united in the same person, or in the same body of magistrates, there can be no liberty; because apprehensions may arise, lest the same monarch or senate should enact tyrannical laws, to execute them in a tyrannical manner.[3]

The Founders constructed the Constitution to stand as a bulwark against the possibility of tyranny by separating powers among three branches of government and ensuring checks and balances among those branches.

Genius. Or, a "quaint" and antiquated concept, depending on your point of view.

Today, laws are conjured all the time without Congress having any involvement whatsoever. For example, the president brandishes unbridled authority to create or change the law when he's displeased with Congress's action or inaction. In fact, during the 2012 election he unabashedly declared, "Where Republicans refuse to cooperate on things that I know are good for the American people, I will continue to look for ways to do it administratively and work around Congress."[4] (If George Washington had threatened such action, I doubt the Constitution would have passed in its current form.)

President Obama has followed through with that threat. As I explained in my paper *Restoring the Rule of Law*:

> [T]he President thinks he can remake entire sectors of the world's biggest and most dynamic economy and use adminis-

trative agencies to displace state law. By one estimate, the President has unilaterally amended Obamacare in 32 separate ways, remaking the Nation's healthcare markets in the process. The President has asserted unilateral authority to regulate virtually every building in the entire United States (all the way down to the corner food mart and drycleaner) in an effort to curb "greenhouse gases." The President has taken executive actions to infringe the Second Amendment rights of millions of lawful gun owners, even though the entire point of the Bill of Rights was to protect Americans from invasions of their liberties. And, but for a lawsuit brought by Texas, the President would have unilaterally ordered the single largest overhaul of the immigration system in our Nation's history.

James Madison, Alexander Hamilton, John Jay and the other Framers of the Constitution would shudder at those results. As shocked as they would be, however, those results are mere symptoms of the disease. What really plagues this Nation is that we have forgotten what it means to be governed by the rule of law, and we have succumbed to the rule of men.[5]

COSTUMES

Halloween has always been a fun tradition at our house. Audrey always looked forward to dressing up and going trick-or-treating. Candidly, Cecilia and I did, too.

Because of my wheelchair, my costume choices could be quite innovative.

One year, we dressed up my wheelchair as a tank. All you could see of me was my head sticking out of the top: I was like Michael

Dukakis in his infamous 1988 campaign video. Another year we dressed up my wheelchair as a shopping cart. We extended the front of the chair with metal rims and tinfoil, and even put grocery bags inside. It was a perfect candy-collecting device.

One Halloween I simply dressed up as a rock. Yeah, I was a "rolling stone."

I'm not the only grown-up who enjoys costumes, but some political leaders in Washington, D.C., like to dress up all year round. Halloween costumes are supposed to be fantasy. Sometimes political leaders dress up as a king and act like it's reality.

Immigration Orders

One example of acting like a king is the way President Obama has wielded executive orders.

For most of his presidency, Barack Obama faced withering criticism from the pro-immigrant community. These groups questioned his refusal to impose reforms that would allow more people to immigrate to the United States—and to provide legal status to the millions of illegal immigrants already here.

President Obama faced unyielding opposition in Congress, which denied him the ability to change the law to accommodate the demands of pro-immigrant groups.

At town halls, speeches, and press events, President Obama was pressured to take action even though Congress, rather than the president, was the government branch charged with making immigration laws. To blunt the criticisms of his inaction on immigration reform, the president rightly reminded audiences that he didn't have the legal authority to unilaterally change the immigration laws.

President Obama reportedly said more than twenty times[6] that he didn't have the authority as president to alter immigration laws. He correctly emphasized that to do so would be the equivalent of acting like a "king" or "emperor," contrary to the Founders' intent.

Here is a sampling of the president's accurate description of his limited power to change immigration laws:

- In 2010, when asked by immigration reform advocates to stop deportations and act alone on providing legal status for the undocumented, President Obama said, "I'm president, I'm not a king. I can't do these things myself."

- In 2011, President Obama provided the most complete and accurate assessment of his legal authority: "With respect to the notion that I can just suspend deportations through executive order, that's just not the case, because there are laws on the books that Congress has passed . . . you know that we've got three branches of government. Congress passes the law. The executive branch's job is to enforce and implement those laws. And then the judiciary has to interpret the laws. There are enough laws on the books by Congress that are very clear in terms of how we have to enforce our immigration system that for me to simply through executive order ignore those congressional mandates would not conform with my appropriate role as president."

- In 2013 he reiterated his limitations: "Well, I think it is important to remind everybody that, as I said I think previously, and I'm not a king. I am the head of the executive branch of government. I'm required to follow the law. And that's what we've done."

- Also in 2013, Obama said, "I'm the president of the United States. I'm not the emperor of the United States. My job is to execute laws that are passed."
- Once again in 2013, the president insisted: "My job in the executive branch is supposed to be to carry out the laws that are passed."[7]

As a constitutional scholar, Barack Obama knew the legal dividing line between presidential and congressional powers. As a pop culture aficionado, he "talked" like he understood the Dirty Harry Rule: "A man's got to know his limitations."

The president was right, of course, because the Constitution *is* crystal clear. Article I, Section 8 gives power to Congress—not the president—to regulate immigration. As President Obama conceded, his constitutional duty is found in Article II, Section 3, which commands the president to "take care that the laws be faithfully executed."

While the president rightly explained his limited power to groups pressing for change, and while Congress did nothing to help solve the problem, America faced a crushing tsunami of new immigrants crossing the border illegally, with Texas facing the brunt of the challenge.

During the spring of 2014, the number of illegal immigrants rushing the Texas border exceeded 10,000 per month. In June 2014 alone, more than 45,000 crossed the border. On average, that was well over one thousand per day.[8]

The sudden spike in illegal immigration was commonly blamed on one thing: the immigrants' perception that once they made it into America, they would be able to stay because the immigration laws were not enforced. What a paradox! America had become the greatest country in world history in large part because we were the ultimate nation of laws rather than of men. And yet immigrants were illegally crossing our border because our federal government abandoned this foundational principle.[9]

America urgently needed to stop the flow of illegal border crossers, and arrest the criminals who had entered illegally—especially those convicted of serious crimes who snuck back into the United States after deportation.

Texas was at the tip of this spear, but our ability to protect our state sovereignty and citizens' safety had been limited by the U.S. Supreme Court and by the Obama administration.

But we were Texas, and we don't kowtow when told we can't do something to protect our state and our safety. So we deployed the National Guard and beefed up the Texas Department of Public Safety to strategically enhance border security.

As then-governor Rick Perry put it, "Drug cartels, human traffickers, individual criminals are exploiting this tragedy for their own criminal opportunities."[10] Texas simply wasn't going to sit idly by.

With the addition of resources from Texas and the U.S. Border Patrol, the illegal crossings began to decline. But the underlying problem of what to do with those already here illegally persisted.

Even with all its blusterous talk, Congress had no appetite to address the problem, despite the fact that it had the sole constitutional authority to tackle the broken immigration system that was burdening Texans with millions, if not billions, of dollars in costs for education, health care, law enforcement, and other services.

With each passing day, one of the most pressing issues in America was left lingering, either because of apathy or, worse, lack of backbone.

Elections Have Consequences

During this time in 2014, I was serving as attorney general and also campaigning for governor of Texas, promising to secure our border. The race drew significant national attention. My opponent, Wendy Davis, was the darling of the liberal left. She filibustered a Texas abortion law designed to protect the unborn, and the safety of women who have abortions. It turned out the filibuster was for naught, because the bill passed the day after Davis's stunt. In the end, though, the hopes of liberals across the country to turn Texas blue were dashed when I was elected on November 4, 2014, by a twenty-point margin.

After the election, I quickly began the transition process from the state's top lawyer to Texas's chief executive. That smooth transition planning to the governorship came to a jolting halt by breaking news splashing across the television screen.

On Thursday, November 20, the president used a prime-time address to announce executive action to give legal status, work permits, and other benefits to five million immigrants in the United States illegally.[11]

In the process, the president lambasted Congress for not acting to change the immigration laws to his liking. The president challenged Congress to "pass a bill" if they didn't like his executive action.

There were two problems with the president's approach. First, it rewrote the Constitution. Under the Constitution, Congress can pass a law and the president can veto it if he wishes. Here the president flipped that process. He said he was going to make new immigration law by altering the current law and told Congress they could veto his action by passing a law.

Another problem undermined the constitutionality of the president's action. Congress had already passed an immigration law— a "comprehensive" one at that. Congress had passed laws signed by former presidents that covered every topic President Obama was trying to alter. The president simply wasn't happy with the law as it existed and brashly rewrote parts of it through his executive action.

One more glaring problem: the president did what he said twenty times he didn't have the legal authority to do. The Constitution hadn't changed. What changed was Barack Obama's willingness to violate it.

The president was acting exactly like the "king" he said he would be if he used executive action to change the immigration laws. The genius of Hamilton, Madison, Franklin, and all the other Founding Fathers was being shredded like a tomato with a Ginsu knife. The very existence of the document that begins with "We the People" was being rewritten by a single person who had assumed kingly powers the Constitution was intended to prevent.

In the end, the king had no clothes. Americans saw through his imperial ways.

Battle Royal

The king had to be stopped. But how? Congress was feckless on this issue, and the president was against us. Once again, as with Obamacare, the states needed to step up and insist constitutional principles be upheld.

I had just fewer than fifty days left to take action as the Texas attorney general—counting the Thanksgiving and Christmas holidays. I needed to organize my gubernatorial operation. But I also knew we had a team of constitutional scholars that was unmatched by any attorney general's or governor's office in America. I had to step up.

My team prepared a sensational brief detailing the constitutional and legal violations of the president's unilateral amnesty executive order. I spoke with my fellow governors and asked them to join a proposed lawsuit against the president. My staff spoke with my attorney general colleagues, with whom I'd fought many legal battles.

For every apprehension raised by my peers about wading into this legal and political battle, we had solid answers.

In just a few weeks, we assembled sixteen states to join our effort. That number quickly expanded to twenty-five. Once again, more than half of America was suing America.

On December 3, 2014, just thirteen days after President Obama announced his amnesty executive action, I rolled up to a podium and announced a lawsuit: *State of Texas v. United States of America*.

It would be the thirty-first lawsuit that I brought against the Obama administration for legal and constitutional violations.

At the press conference, I emphasized two points: First, our immigration system is broken. Second, the Constitution prescribes immigration policy be fixed by *Congress*, not by presidential decree.

I described how the president clearly violated our constitutional structure. He unilaterally *suspended* significant parts of existing immigration laws. Then, in a moment of candor, the president confessed: "I just took an action to change the law." [12] The president has no power to do either of these acts.

I explained that the president's executive action violated his promise to the American people to "take care that the Laws be faithfully executed." This isn't loose language to embroider the Constitution. The ability of the president to dispense with laws was *specifically considered* and rejected at the Constitutional Convention.

The Take Care Clause was inserted into the Constitution to prevent *this very type* of conduct by a president. The president's job is to execute the laws, not "change" them or "suspend" parts of laws passed by Congress.

In addition to violating the Constitution, I also explained that the president's executive action violated a law called the Administrative Procedure Act. That act requires a federal agency like the Department of Homeland Security to provide notice to the public about a rule change, and provide an opportunity for the public to comment on it. Because that didn't happen, the proposed rule change was invalid.

AWKWARD

My lawsuit against the president was filed on the first Wednesday in December 2014, in my final month as attorney general.

Weeks earlier, I had already accepted an invitation to join with other newly elected governors to meet with the president and his staff at the White House. That meeting was on the first Friday of December, two days *after* I filed the lawsuit.

As Audrey would say, *awkward!*

The formalities began with other new governors and me having lunch with Vice President Joe Biden. We then met with cabinet members like Secretary of Health and Human Services Sylvia Mathews Burwell, Environmental Protection Agency director Gina McCarthy, and Secretary of Education Arne Duncan.

Next we were escorted to the Roosevelt Room for a briefing by the president's key advisors.

The Roosevelt Room is connected by a large doorway to the

Oval Office. After our briefing, the doors opened, and the president walked to the door threshold to greet us and shook hands with each governor as we passed through the door to the Oval Office.

I was last in the procession.

For the past forty-eight hours the president's team had been feverishly responding to questions about my lawsuit challenging the executive amnesty order, and now this new "cowboy governor" shows up at the Oval Office threshold.

As I approached President Obama to shake his hand, I thought I'd have a little fun. So I shook his hand as he graciously yet tensely said, "Welcome, Governor Abbott."

"Mr. President," I said, "you're causing me a hard time back home."

I could feel the tension increase. "How's that?" he asked with a puzzled look. I imagined he was thinking, *God, I thought Governor Perry was bad, now I've got to deal with this guy.*

Unbeknownst to the president, my daughter, always curious about what I was doing, had googled the president before my trip and came across his presentation at the White House Correspondents' Association Dinner. She disagrees with the president politically but thought his jokes were hilarious.

I answered the president's question, "I have a daughter one year older than Malia, and I gotta tell you, my daughter thinks you're a whole lot funnier than I am."

Immediately he smiled and the tension faded. He slapped me on the back and said: "Those girls, they'll break your heart."

We all moved to the Oval Office with less tension in the air. The president took his seat in front of the familiar fireplace, while the new governors sat on two couches, one to the right and one to the left of the president.

I searched for an open space where I could park my wheelchair. I found one on the opposite side of the room from the president, immediately in front of his desk.

But the president said, "Hey, Greg"—now I'm Greg—"come sit over here by me?"

I couldn't say no.

I rolled into place to his immediate right, and as soon as I locked my wheels, the doors to the Rose Garden burst open. Thirty photographers rushed in and started flashing like a swarm of paparazzi.

I'm thinking, I just got played. Two days ago I sued the president. Now pictures are being taken with us side by side. *Man, this isn't going to sell well in Texas.*

In about sixty seconds, the flash mob left, and we returned to our discussion.

The president looked to his left to the newly elected governor from Rhode Island, Gina Raimondo, and asked, "How are things going in your state?"

Before answering the question, the governor interjected a comment along the lines of "Mr. President, I want to personally thank you for coming to Rhode Island to campaign for me—it made such a difference."

After the unannounced flash mob, I figured all was fair game. And besides, everyone was a little looser by now.

Before the president could respond to the Rhode Island governor, I spread my arms widely, signaling disbelief, and interrupted. "What?! You didn't come to Texas to campaign!"

The president gently reached over and placed his hand on my left arm and quipped with a big grin, "Greg, I don't think it would have helped."

Just as quickly I replied: "Oh, Mr. President . . . it would have helped." Everyone in the room got the joke and enjoyed a good laugh.

After some more conversation, it was time to adjourn. As President Obama got up from his chair, he put his hand on my arm again and, with that same wry smile we've all seen on TV, asked a question.

"So . . . Greg . . . Can I get you to drop that lawsuit?"

BORDERLAND

The lawsuit was filed in federal court in Brownsville, Texas— ground zero along the Rio Grande River, where illegal crossings are commonplace. That region had two federal judges: one a Clinton appointee, the other a George W. Bush appointee named Andrew Hanen. Our case was assigned to Judge Hanen.

Quick research revealed that Judge Hanen was no friend of sloppy immigration practices. A year before our case was filed, he issued an order that should be mandatory reading for Americans.

As opposed to the secondhand interpretations you read in the paper or watch on TV, Judge Hanen issued a federal court order, based on facts in a case in his court, that describes in detail America's broken immigration system. Because I want you to see what a federal judge has to say about our broken border, I have included Judge Hanen's order in the Appendix to this book.

To give you a flavor of what he says, I'll quote a few lines:

- "The DHS [Department of Homeland Security], instead of enforcing our border security laws, actually assisted the criminal conspiracy in achieving its illegal goals."

- "The DHS has simply chosen not to enforce the United States' border security laws."
- "[T]he DHS should cease telling the citizens of the United States that it is enforcing our border security laws because it is clearly not. Even worse, it is helping those who violate these laws."

Despite the typical pundit predictions that our case was meritless and filed only for political theater, we won a quick victory in Judge Hanen's court. Even more meaningful, his order put a complete halt across the entire country to President Obama's amnesty-granting executive order.

Finally, a judge who applied the law. One man—the president—can try to change the law. Another man—a federal judge—can correct the executive overreach. That is the way the legal system is supposed to work.

The lower-court victory was followed by a win at the U.S. Court of Appeals. Importantly, the president's signature immigration order has remained halted across America, proving the powerful role states can play in shaping our country.

As this book is going to print, the Supreme Court has agreed to hear the case but hasn't yet reached a decision. If the justices rule for the Obama administration, they will have trashed Article I of the Constitution, which gives Congress—and only Congress—the authority to regulate immigration.

A ruling for the Obama administration would also virtually erase Article II of the Constitution, which prevents the president from making or rewriting laws and instead mandates that he "take Care that the Laws be faithfully executed."

If the Supreme Court concludes that the president can rewrite a law, that result should finally spur Americans to get off the sidelines and join in the process of applying Article V—the constitutional tool the Founders gave "the People" to correct such abuses.

The rule of law is what makes America unique. Once we decide, by action or inaction, that leaders get to do whatever "feels" right, we will descend into chaos and tyranny. We can't let that happen.

REAGAN WAS RIGHT

President Reagan foreshadowed the need for these reforms in repeated urgings to control the gaping growth of government. He summarized the challenges that had grown from a government unhinged from the people and the need to control it. He reminded us, "We are a nation that has a government—not the other way around."

Like the Founders, President Reagan was prescient about a government run amok.

Reagan was equally prophetic about the solution to the problem. He rightly observed: "our government has no power except that granted to it by the people. It is time to check and reverse the growth of government which shows signs of having grown beyond the consent of the governed."

Although President Reagan predicted the problems and envisioned solutions, he, himself, proved that even a president who robustly rejects an overreaching federal government cannot summon the reforms that allow the people to control government. Despite a conservative record that matched his rhetorical bravado to constrain the size and scope of government, the problem is far worse today than it was during the Reagan administration.

The Reagan example proves an essential point: the true answer to government run amok cannot be found in any single leader whose tenure is limited and whose effectiveness can be eroded over time.

Instead, the solution must be made of sterner stuff. The fix must be ingrained in our governing document, the Constitution itself, in order to remove unintended and harmful powers from the hands of the president, Congress, and the courts.

The Constitution, not elected leaders or unelected bureaucrats, has always been the premier guardian of the people. We must fortify the Constitution, using the very means the document provides, to truly protect the people from the mischief of misguided leaders.

THE FORCE OF LAW

In 1776, Thomas Paine stated in his pamphlet *Common Sense* that "in America, the law is king." Four years later, John Adams wrote this principle into the Massachusetts Constitution, seeking to establish "a government of laws and not of men."

Laws are the voice of the people, speaking through their elected representatives.

As you look through the history of the United States, and some of the injustices that have occurred, it was the Constitution that gave us the power to correct those inequities. Whether it be ending slavery, or giving all women the right to vote, the Constitution provided the mechanism for change.

We must never turn away from the mechanisms of change provided by the Founders to ensure that America remains a government of laws, not of men.

If we are going to restore people's faith in government, then the government has to behave according to law. The success of this nation depends on it.

By issuing his executive amnesty order, Barack Obama moved away from being the president envisioned by the Founders. Instead he put on the costume of a fiat-wielding tyrant the Founders fought to prevent. It's our fault if we do nothing about it.

Six

Power and Problems

Freedom is never more than one generation away from extinction.
It has to be fought for and defended by each generation.
—RONALD REAGAN

Because broken vertebrae crushed my spinal cord, my legs are paralyzed. So when it comes to walking, I simply can't move.

That's a fair description of Congress when it comes to its obligation to move legislation the nation desperately needs. America is facing some extraordinarily consequential issues with no substantial action from Congress. They are simply paralyzed.

For example, because the Constitution gives Congress responsibility to pass laws regulating immigration, it has the constitutional power to pass laws to secure our porous border. And yet, because of Congress's inaction to improve an outdated system, thousands of immigrants illegally flow into our country—every week.

Even worse, Congress knows that some of those immigrants are refugees from terrorist-sponsored nations. The FBI director and the director of national intelligence explained that they lack the ability to vet the security of those refugees. Consequently, Congress's inaction to secure our border and ports of entry exposes Americans to life-and-death threats.

With the lives of Americans across the country on the line, you'd expect Congress to immediately act to protect us. And yet the issue of protecting America's sovereignty and our collective security has lingered for years in Congress, with the dangers growing worse by the day.

For example, in early 2016, a refugee from Iraq was arrested in Texas for plotting to explode deadly bombs at the Galleria, a high-end mall in Houston.[1] This national discussion is no longer theoretical. We face very real threats because the president is allowing these potentially dangerous refugees into our country and Congress does nothing to stop it. While various members of Congress offer bills to address these challenges, nothing gets passed, and problems aren't solved.

More broadly, Congress's paralysis has empowered the other two branches of government to exercise powers they weren't intended to have. The Framers of the Constitution purposefully created three branches of government—the legislative, executive, and judicial—to serve as checks and balances on power wielded by each other branch. Congress has seemingly abandoned this role and, with some rare exceptions, has acquiesced in the unconstitutional actions by the executive and judicial branches.

For example, Congress can and should override the unconstitutional overreaches by the president and the administrative agencies in the executive branch. States should not have to ride to the rescue on issues like the Obamacare overreach, or agencies like the EPA acting beyond the scope of their authority.

Congress has the power to rein in the executive branch by voting down any—or every—proposal of a defiant president or act to override constitutionally dubious executive orders. And, as both Alexander Hamilton and James Madison made clear, Congress wields the ultimate power of the purse to check unconstitutional straying by the executive branch.

Madison was particularly emphatic: "This power over the purse may, in fact, be regarded as the most complete and effectual weapon with which any constitution can arm the immediate representatives of the people, for obtaining a redress of every grievance, and for carrying into effect every just and salutary measure."[2]

Madison would be shocked to see how meekly Congress has abandoned this "weapon."

Similarly, Congress has the power to override a Supreme Court that increasingly rewrites acts of Congress and freely amends the Constitution to add words, phrases, and concepts found nowhere in the document, or in the Founders' intent. Yet that congressional power has atrophied from nonuse.

In the end, Congress has become paralyzed because it has shown no spine to check the unconstitutional overreach by the other two branches.

PURSE STRINGS

Maybe Congress hasn't followed Madison's advice to use the power of the purse to control the other branches because it can't control its own use of the purse when it comes to spending your money.

Take a moment away from this book and click on the Web site www.GregAbbott.com/book for a link to the U.S. Debt Clock. This kinetic Web page shows the national debt and a host of other financial items, in real time. At first it's fascinating and captivating to look at. All those colorful numbers moving so fast. It makes you feel like a kid in an arcade.

Then reality sinks in. The people responsible for those debt numbers have been acting like kids in an arcade. Their irresponsible and unrestrained spending has sunk us $19 *trillion* in debt. That's almost $60,000 for every man, woman, and child in America.

It would take years to pay off that debt, if they were trying. The problem is, they aren't even trying. As the Debt Clock shows, Congress continues to spend more money than the country takes in. We are borrowing a million dollars a minute.

The Constitution gives Congress the power to raise and spend money. Their reckless approach to spending your money does more than exceed the authority that was given to Congress in the Constitution. It's one of the most dangerous threats to our future liberty.

I know some politicians talk about the dangers of our national debt. But few explain the real-world effects in ways that grab the attention of Americans across the political spectrum.

With each additional dollar in debt, we are less able to provide for the roads and schools we need, and less certain are the promises made about Social Security and Medicare. In 2013 alone, the United States paid its lenders $222 billion.[3] That's $222 billion that could have gone to schools, or veterans, or . . . you—as a reduction in the tax you pay.

Instead, that money is being used to pay our lenders, the largest of which is China.

Maybe more ominously, our national security itself becomes more at risk each day we grow further in debt. America's debt weakens our ability to amass the weapons, intelligence, and personnel needed to defend against an increasingly antagonistic world.

The America of tomorrow will be a mere shadow of today unless we compel Congress to get a grip on its reckless spending now.

Warren Buffett, the iconic investor and chronic Democrat, offered an idea: "I could end the deficit in five minutes," he said. "You just pass a law that says that anytime there is a deficit of more than three percent of GDP all sitting members of Congress are ineligible for reelection."

One can dream.

LIZARDS OLD AND NEW

Just as pesky as Congress spending your money is Congress passing laws that cost you money—laws that elevate the lives of lizards, smelt, and spiders above the future of mothers, fathers, and children.

Texas is the home of, among other things, oil. A good chunk of it is in the West Texas area called the Permian Basin.

The oil in that ground is more than a product you'll use one day. It is the font of thousands upon thousands of jobs that pay for backpacks and bicycles, hamburgers and ham sandwiches, winter coats and summer sandals, and homes for people to live in.

The Permian Basin is also home of the dunes sagebrush lizard, which enjoys the desertlike sand dunes of the basin area. The lizard, as tough as Texas, has coexisted with Permian Basin oil production for decades.

That relationship was rudely interrupted by the federal government.

Congress created the Endangered Species Act, a law viewed by some as the nation's most powerful environmental law. If land is designated as falling under the act, virtually all human activity on that land is either prohibited or subject to substantial regulation.

The Endangered Species Act's "Enforcer" is the U.S. Fish and Wildlife Service. In 2010, that agency proposed the dunes sagebrush lizard to be listed as "endangered."

For every employer, worker, or property owner, the word *endangered* conjures a sensation like fingernails screeching across a blackboard.

The proposed listing of the lizard as endangered immediately put thousands of jobs, and billions of dollars in economic activity, at risk.

The president of the Permian Basin Petroleum Association, Ben Shepperd, explained the economic impact: "The wolf at the door is the lizard; we're concerned listing it would shut down drilling activity for a minimum of two years and as many as five years while the service determines what habitat is needed for the lizard. That means no drilling, no seismic surveys, no roads built, no electric lines." [4]

LIMITATIONS

I was the Texas attorney general at the time. I told my team that we would form a Lizard Litigation Unit if necessary to combat what seemed to be an egregious regulatory overreach by the U.S. Fish and Wildlife Service.

For me, the issue was even larger than the potential lost jobs and economic destruction. My concern, once again, focused on the destruction of human liberty caused by a federal government exceeding its constitutional authority.

Every branch of government has authority—and constitutional

limitations on that authority. Congress can't pass just any law it wants. The Founders knew better than to give it such unlimited authority. Instead, the Constitution limits Congress to passing laws that fall under its "enumerated powers," found in Article I.

Congress based the Endangered Species Act—and thus the U.S. Fish and Wildlife's ability to enforce it—on the Commerce Clause in the Constitution. That's the same Commerce Clause that members of Congress thought they based Obamacare on—that is, until Chief Justice Roberts ruled that Obamacare was a tax.

The Commerce Clause empowers Congress to regulate commercial activity among the states, not activity inside one state only. Putting aside the issue of whether a lizard that no one buys or sells is commerce, the hard truth for the U.S. Fish and Wildlife Service was that the lizard didn't cross state lines. It remained happily burrowed in Texas's sand dunes.

Although the Endangered Species Act had been upheld under similar circumstances in other states, I believe the Fish and Wildlife agency realized that if they moved forward to officially list the Texas lizard, the thing that would be truly endangered was the Endangered Species Act itself.

They knew we were prepared to take this case to the U.S. Supreme Court and strike down the Endangered Species Act as an unconstitutional expansion of the Commerce Clause.

In 2012, the U.S. Fish and Wildlife Service decided not to list the lizard as endangered. The Texas economy, our citizens, and the dunes sagebrush lizard have lived happily ever after, without the meddling of the federal government.

Unfortunately, the same cannot be said for how Congress's Endangered Species Act has trampled Americans' property rights and pocketbooks in other states. A fly, some fish, a toad, even cave bugs—and the property surrounding them—have been protected under the act.

For example, much to the economic damage to Californians, the Ninth Circuit Federal Court of Appeals upheld an endangered species listing of the delta smelt, a small fish endemic to California.

The listing was challenged by the Pacific Legal Foundation on the grounds that the fish was a "purely intrastate species" with "no commercial value" and thus could not be regulated under the Commerce Clause, which doesn't apply to only intrastate activity.[5]

The Ninth Circuit disagreed with this plain reading of the Constitution. Instead it ruled that "Congress has the power to regulate purely intrastate activity as long as the activity is being regulated under a general regulatory scheme that bears a substantial relationship to interstate commerce."[6]

That's Latin for the phrase "Congress can regulate whatever it wants."

The overbearing use of the Endangered Species Act has spawned a new group called PETPO. That's the People for the Ethical Treatment of Property Owners. That group won a lawsuit in federal court that challenged U.S. Fish and Wildlife's ability to list a species under the act if it neither crosses state lines nor has economic value. That case will remain in the appellate swamp for a while.

But the PETPO case represents a turning point. Maybe a *returning* point to where the country was intended to be oriented since its founding. It returns the focus to the rights given to the people of this country under the Constitution, and restores the limits the Constitution places on Congress's ability to regulate OUR lives.[7]

DODD-FRANK AND YOUR BANK

Weeks after Barack Obama was elected in November 2008, Wall Street continued to sputter, reeling from what was dubbed the "Great Recession." Rahm Emanuel, President Obama's new chief of staff, seized on the panic by saying: "You never want a serious crisis to go to waste." [8]

Such faux-wisdom can lead to arrogant policy decisions that wreak havoc on Americans. That's exactly what happened when the president and Congress cobbled together their reforms for Wall Street and the banking industry.

The Constitution is especially vulnerable during times of economic distress. By far the most substantial modifications to the Constitution since the Bill of Rights occurred under the administration of Franklin D. Roosevelt during the Great Depression, with an assist from a compliant, and panicked, Congress. Unlike the Bill of Rights however, FDR's constitutional tinkering did not go through the Article V amendment process.

Just like during the Great Depression, the 2008 financial crisis rushed Washington lawmakers to craft legislation, *purportedly* to curtail risky practices that had precipitated the financial collapse. The Obama administration and Congress seized on the FDR model and hammered out laws, rules, and regulations that were both indecipherable and constitutionally suspect.

They created the 2010 Dodd-Frank Wall Street Reform and Consumer Protection Act. Rather than simply correcting the banking practices that contributed to the financial crisis, Congress embraced Rahm Emanuel's thesis to not let the crisis go to waste. They used the opportunity to impose a colossal regulatory regime that expanded government mandates on a range of products and activities, such as insurance and debit card purchases.

Not only did the law not effectively address the problems, but many argue that it made them worse. Dodd-Frank was intended to prevent banks from being too big to fail, and, hence, avoid the necessity of government bailouts. Instead, the high cost and heavy hand by which the regulations are imposed are leading to the opposite result: eliminating banks that are too small to succeed.[9]

Dodd-Frank not only burdens financial institutions with an unwieldy labyrinth of regulations; it also chokes lending that is desperately needed to fuel our economic engine. If you've applied for a loan or home mortgage in recent years, or if you've tried to borrow money to grow your business, you've heard about, and felt, the unpleasant effects of this law and its Pandora's box of regulations.

Dodd-Frank has been called Dodd-Frankenstein for good reason: it created a convoluted web of governance that produced more uncertainty than solutions. Congress felt an urgent need to show America that it was acting. Unfortunately, as is often the case, Congress overreacted.

The good news was that brand-new agencies like the Consumer Financial Protection Bureau and the Financial Stability Oversight Council were created. Okay, I'm being sarcastic. It's a coping mechanism for government dysfunction.

The bad news was that new agencies were created. And the regulatory power of agencies like the Securities and Exchange Commission, the Federal Reserve, and others was expanded.

Congress handed the reins to rule our financial markets to unelected, unaccountable bureaucrats.

What could possibly go wrong?

Institutional Idiocy

Putting aside the debatable pros and cons of Dodd-Frank, my concern about the law had nothing to do with the reforms. Had the law mandated that banks give away free toasters, we still would have fought it. Once again, I was shocked by the ease with which Congress abandoned constitutional principles in an effort to score political points.

In 2013, Texas joined several other states and private parties, including a Texas bank, to overturn the Dodd-Frank law because its very framework was completely unconstitutional.

The lawsuit asserted three primary claims.

First, the Consumer Financial Protection Bureau (CFPB), created by Dodd-Frank, violates constitutional separation-of-powers principles. Congress effectively gives unbounded power to the CFPB to regulate financial institutions and then insulates that agency from meaningful checks by the legislative, executive, and judicial branches.

For example, the CFPB director can't be fired by Congress or the president, regardless of how whimsically or heavy-handedly he makes and enforces regulations. Congress actually infused unaccountability into this law.

To make matters worse, Congress abdicated its "power of the purse" over the CFPB by authorizing that agency to fund itself by unilaterally claiming money from the Federal Reserve System. The law explicitly *prohibits* the House and Senate appropriations committees from even attempting to "review" the CFPB's self-funded budget. James Madison is surely turning over in his grave.

We argued that by delegating almost unlimited power to the CFPB, by eliminating Congress's own "power of the purse" over the CFPB, by eliminating the president's power to remove the CFPB director at will, and by limiting the courts' judicial review of the CFPB's actions and legal interpretations, Dodd-Frank violates the Constitution's separation of powers.

Second, the lawsuit explained that Congress also violated the separation of powers by creating another new entity called the Financial Stability Oversight Council, a/k/a the FSOC. (By the way, Congress doesn't speak English. They have their own coded language that uses an alphabet-soup aggregation of letters.)

Congress gave this new group the sweeping and unprecedented power to choose which *nonbank* financial companies should be designated as too big to fail. Essentially, Congress embedded into the law the power for unelected and unaccountable bureaucrats to pick winners and losers in the financial sector.

Third, by giving the U.S. Treasury secretary broad and unilateral authority to order the liquidation of financial businesses with little or no advance warning, under cover of mandatory secrecy, and without meaningful legislative, executive, or judicial oversight, Dodd-Frank violates the separation of powers and also the Fifth Amendment protection against having your property taken "without due process of law."

Under this part of Dodd-Frank, unelected federal bureaucrats can liquidate financial institutions in which states like Texas invest taxpayer dollars. States—and their taxpayers—can be denied due process rights by having their taxpayer-funded investments liquidated by federal officials.

It gets worse.

When the Treasury secretary decides to liquidate a business, a court must conduct a hearing and issue a decision *within twenty-four hours.*

This court hearing must be conducted on a "strictly confidential basis, and without any prior public disclosure." This means that Texas, or any state, could have its investments swept away in twenty-four hours without ever even knowing about it.

In short, Congress mandated secret proceedings by unelected bureaucrats to liquidate someone's business, and unilaterally decide how the spoils will be divided.

Is that what America has come to? Is that what Alexander Hamilton and James Madison designed?

SO FAR, SO BAD

Later in 2013, the trial court dismissed our case as premature. It concluded that Texas and the other parties bringing the lawsuit hadn't yet been harmed.

In other words, the court was saying that banks, individuals, and even states had to wait until financial losses were racked up before bringing suit. Isn't that what Dodd-Frank was intended to protect against? It seemed the court was requiring the very thing the law was intended to prevent: financial loss.

No wonder Americans think that courts and Congress lack common sense.

Congress abandoned the Constitution to create a federal financial dictatorship. And courts have aided Congress by refusing to enforce the Fifth Amendment right to due process of law.

The Constitution was purposefully constructed to protect against these very evils. Clearly, that purpose is being undermined and eroded with each act of Congress.

There's a reason why the public's perception of Congress remains so low. When legislators should act, they seem paralyzed. When Congress should restrain itself, it exceeds its constitutional authority and simply makes bad problems worse.

It's up to the American people to stand up and take charge of their government. Because freedom is in our DNA.

Seven

Our Original Design

. . . to secure these rights, Governments are instituted among Men, deriving their just powers from the consent of the governed . . .
—PREAMBLE TO THE DECLARATION OF INDEPENDENCE

We are designed to walk—it's in our DNA.

This process begins by rolling over, crawling, standing, and in a flash we graduate into a new world of freedom as our first steps begin.

Few moments generate independence in a child like gaining the ability to walk. Once a child begins walking, they can explore the world around them and move toward areas that interest them.

Not until my accident did I fully appreciate this freedom. Then, suddenly, at every turn, there seemed to be obstacles.

DESIGNED TO OVERCOME

The good news is that we're also designed to overcome obstacles. Deep within each of us lies the ability to conquer our circumstances.

During months of hospitalization, surgeries, and rehab, I came to grips with two realities about life:

First, you never know when a tree is going to fall on you.

Second, my back was broken, but not my spirit.

In going on to become a Texas Supreme Court justice, state attorney general, and now governor of Texas, I realized that our lives are not defined by how we're challenged. Instead, they're determined by how we respond to life's challenges.

It's the same ideal that's infused in your life, and in America's history.

The principle of charting a course to overcome challenges has permeated our country from its very beginning. It's the crux of our Declaration of Independence, which I read and reread during my hospital stay.

That principle is being tested in our nation, just as it was for me. My paralysis and loss of independence are a striking parallel to the condition of America today.

America was born with a Declaration of Independence that infused our societal DNA with freedom. The decades following the Declaration were years of growth and expansion that flowed from the greatest governing document ever to exist: the U.S. Constitution.

But America has become increasingly paralyzed. With each passing year, our upward mobility is more challenging because of one overarching obstacle: our independence is being sapped by a centralized government that erodes our constitutional liberties and crushes the aspirations that elevated this great nation.

All three branches of our federal government are virtual co-conspirators in this demise.

The executive branch increasingly issues executive orders that circumvent the lawmaking process, and unaccountable bureaucrats are making the rule of law, rather than the legislative branch as designed by the Constitution.

Congress has abandoned its role as the architect of the people's policy and has devolved into dysfunction. It has joined with the executive branch to saddle America with choking regulations and insurmountable debt.

Instead of applying laws as written, the judiciary has assumed the role of an unaccountable superlegislature, freely rewriting laws and even altering the Constitution itself without the approval of the American people.

These departures from our original design explain, in part, why each passing year our dreams appear further from our reach and harder to grasp. Our economy, our global authority, and, most significantly, our individual liberties are becoming increasingly paralyzed by governmental control.

DESIGNED TO THRIVE

Imagine the quintessential Main Street, in the town of your youth. The promise and strength of America were reflected in thousands of these streets across the country. But are these images becoming more or less common today?

Your favorite restaurant on Main Street is closed. Mom-and-pop shops are either abandoned or turned into thrift stores or food banks.

There has been much talk about the plight of small-town America—as well as big-city America. Pundits blame big-box stores and cheap imports for declines. But there's a bigger, silent, culprit at work—federal regulation.

The cloud of federal regulation has become so large over the American economy, many people have forgotten what the sun looks like. But there's still hope.

When federal and state governments follow the Constitution and offer lawful policies that establish fair and predictable rules, citizens feel confident about the future. This confidence, in turn, spurs investment in new ideas and creates jobs.

When the manufacturing plant down the road is successful, people drive their new cars to support local businesses. When farmers and ranchers thrive, they take their kids out to dinner in restaurants filled with other prospering families. When communities are free to grow, schools can excel.

Thriving local economies create a thriving regional economy, and people start more small businesses. This is the Main Street that made America great. Growth is in our DNA.

America is an idea, and a place, where big dreams and hard work can propel a person to success. But there are growing barriers impeding our freedom to succeed—freedom that was once taken for granted.

Yes, our government is broken, and our country is facing substantial challenges. The same questions that have been put to every generation of Americans are now put to us: How are we going to respond? Are we going to allow the fate of this country to be diminished by these challenges? Or are we, just like our predecessors, up to the task of overcoming these challenges by charting a course for an even better future?

Liberty and Justice for All

There are striking parallels between my loss of independence and the erosion of freedom in our country. Similarly uncanny is the resemblance between the complaints lodged by the Founders and the concerns felt by Americans today.

Just look at a few phrases from the Declaration of Independence and see how they compare with our current condition.

The Declaration of Independence begins:

> WHEN in the Course of human Events, it becomes necessary for one People to dissolve the Political Bands which have connected them with another, and to assume among the Powers of the Earth, the separate and equal Station to which the Laws of Nature and of Nature's God entitle them, a decent Respect to the Opinions of Mankind requires that they should declare the causes which impel them to the Separation.

The modern version of this would echo the declaration of the Founders: There comes a time when it is necessary for the people of this country to take action to *restore* the bonds that have united us, declare the causes which compel those actions, and put forth solutions which address the core problems.

The Preamble continues:

> WE hold these Truths to be self-evident, that all Men are created equal, that they are endowed by their Creator with certain unalienable Rights, that among these are Life, Liberty and the pursuit of Happiness. —That to secure these Rights, Gov-

ernments are instituted among Men, deriving their just Powers
from the Consent of the Governed . . .

Those *truths* are just as self-evident today as they were in 1776.
What is different about today, though, is the extent the country has
drifted from the last ten words: "*deriving their just powers from the consent of the governed.*" Contrary to our original design, the consent of
the governed is often ignored in the modern-era federal government
pursuit of power.

> that whenever any Form of Government becomes destruc-
> tive of these Ends, it is the Right of the People to alter or to abol-
> ish it, and to institute new Government, laying its Foundation
> on such Principles and organizing its Powers in such Form, as to
> them shall seem most likely to effect their Safety and Happiness.

The federal government certainly has become destructive to our
unalienable rights. But, today, we don't need to abolish our form of
government. Instead, it would be more accurate to say: When our
government becomes destructive to the truths articulated in the
Declaration of Independence and the Constitution, it remains the
right of the people to bring government in line with those truths.

> Prudence, indeed, will dictate that Governments long estab-
> lished should not be changed for light and transient Causes. . . .
> But when a long Train of Abuses and Usurpations, pursuing in-
> variably the same Object evinces a Design to reduce them under
> absolute Despotism, it is their Right, it is their Duty, to throw
> off such Government, and to provide new Guards for their
> future Security.

Again, the recurring truth is evident: We should not change the Constitution for light or transient reasons. But it is just as true today as it was in 1776 that when a long list of "abuses and usurpations" has occurred, it is our right and "Duty, to throw off such Government, and to provide new Guards for their future Security."

REPEATED PETITIONS AND REPEATED INJURY

> In every stage of these Oppressions we have Petitioned for Redress in the most humble Terms: Our repeated Petitions have been answered only by repeated Injury.

Similarly, with our modern-day grievances, we have repeatedly "Petitioned for Redress" from the executive and legislative branches of government. And, repeatedly, we have sought relief from the judicial branch.

For example, as Texas attorney general, I sued the federal government thirty-four times. Not because I wanted to, but because I had to protect constitutional principles. Often these lawsuits were joined by states across the country; sometimes by more than half of the states.

Countless other times, as governor and as attorney general, I have petitioned the president and Congress for relief from an overreaching federal government or from a government failing to fulfill its constitutional obligations.

Our modern-day petitions—just as the Founders experienced—often go unanswered or the problem complained of just gets worse.

The need to fight for our freedom has never been greater. Our country has always faced threats from foreign enemies, but today we're now also seeing unprecedented threats to our liberty from our own federal government.

Their Grievances Are Our Grievances

The Declaration of Independence goes on to list dozens of grievances the patriots had with the king and government of Great Britain.

Americans today could also provide a lengthy list of their grievances about the federal government. I'll mention just a few, focusing particularly on grievances about which I have personally petitioned the government for relief.

Freedom of speech protected by the First Amendment is threatened by an IRS that targets groups and individuals based on political ideology.

Freedom of religion protected by the First Amendment is threatened by laws that coerce people of faith to violate their conscience.

The right to keep and bear arms protected by the Second Amendment is threatened by both the executive and legislative branches every time a criminal uses a gun to commit a crime.

Fifth Amendment rights have been compromised by laws like Dodd-Frank and weakened by Court decisions, like *Kelo v. City of New London*, that allowed government to take your home and give it to private developers.

The Tenth Amendment has been diluted and abandoned by all three branches of the federal government. As a result, the Founders' guarantee in the Tenth Amendment to protect the states and individuals from an overreaching federal government has been gutted.

Private property rights are threatened by federal agencies like the Environmental Protection Agency, which is now attempting to regulate ditches and ponds on private property.

The federal government has abandoned its primary responsibility to secure our safety and sovereignty by failing, and even refusing, to secure our national border, contrary to the clear laws of this nation. Responsibility for regulating immigration given to Congress under the Constitution has been hijacked by the executive branch, which has chosen to abandon enforcing the law the way Congress wrote it.

A federal judge ruled that rather than enforcing our border security laws, the executive branch has "actually assisted the criminal conspiracy" of helping those who violate them.

Contrary to the Tenth Amendment, the federal government has forced states to bear costs related to law enforcement, education, and health care arising from the federal government's failure and refusal to secure our border.

The federal government has sunk this nation into a record amount of debt and has saddled future generations with entitlement expenditures and debt financing that may make it impossible to overcome our debt without compromising our liberty.

The federal government has forced Americans to buy products and services against their will.

The federal government has violated the Tenth Amendment by forcing states to comply with federally established education standards that are found nowhere in the Constitution in order for states to receive their share of education funding.

Both the federal government and the federal judiciary have effectively, and illegally, "amended" the Constitution by engrafting onto it new rights and duties, without using the constitutionally prescribed method to amend it.

I could go on—and you can probably add to the list, too—but you get the idea. We have a federal government that has come unhinged from the promise of the Constitution and has provoked grievances like those made by the Founders.

THE COMMON THREAD

With all these issues, and dozens more, there is a common thread with the challenges the Founders faced: the time for "protestations and supplications" is over. To paraphrase the signers of the Declaration of Independence: *Been there, done that.*

Now it is time to act to ensure our liberty is protected.

Just as I pieced my life back together after losing my independence, and eventually went on to achieve even greater goals, so must our nation piece itself back together from the dismantling of our liberties.

Americans today have every inherent right that the Founders had. We deserve the same freedoms they sought—and eventually attained. The only remaining question: do we have the guts and determination the founding patriots had to stand for principle?

Or, have we collectively grown too weak to impose our will, or too apathetic to chart our course?

The good news is that to steer our nation back onto our constitutional course we don't have to *"mutually pledge to each other our Lives, our Fortunes and our sacred Honor"* as the Founders did. We don't need to take up arms to fight against the federal government. Instead, the Founders handed us the ammunition we need. They loaded it in the Constitution itself.

They clearly understood we would need to mend the Constitution from the wear and tear caused by the government. They not only anticipated that need, but they also made it clear that states and citizens would play a pivotal role in that mending process.

After starting with Article I of the Constitution, which establishes the legislative branch of government, the Founders added Articles II and III, which create the executive and judicial branches of government.

Article IV of the Constitution deals with the relationship between the states and the federal government, and relationships among the states.

Then, before going any further, the Founders purposefully added Article V to the Constitution—the tool to fix a broken federal government. This tool is the amendment process.

CONVENTIONAL THINKING

After the Constitutional Convention in 1787, Ben Franklin was asked by a bystander in Philadelphia, "Well, Doctor, what have we got—a Republic or a Monarchy?"

Franklin replied, "A Republic—if you can keep it."

Every generation of Americans has faced Franklin's challenge. Do we have the will to keep our republic?

Two centuries after Franklin, Ronald Reagan added more to Ben Franklin's point: "Freedom is never more than one generation away from extinction. We didn't pass it to our children in the bloodstream. It must be fought for, protected and handed on for them to do the same."

The good news is that Franklin and the other Founders knew that if the three branches of government strayed, there was a fourth group to rein them in. That group is identified in the first three words of the Constitution: "We the People." The Founders knew that citizens are the ultimate defense against an overbearing federal government.

TILTED GOVERNMENT

As I learned the hard way from the "tilt table" in the ICU, if we stay flat on our backs for long enough, we forget what it's like to be upright.

The same goes for the freedoms we see slipping away. We can't simply lie down and accept the nonstop assault on the Constitution. We don't have to accept a "new normal." Yes, rising up may seem impossible, and dizzyingly difficult. But the alternative is worse: atrophy and oppression.

The alarming tragedy of our broken government is that the person left out of the equation is . . . you! Your freedoms are diminishing while officials in Washington, D.C., become more and more empowered.

Our broken government is not a Republican problem, nor is it a Democrat problem, or any other political party's problem. It's an American problem. And we cannot allow the future of America to be defined by this challenge. Instead we must ensure our future is determined by how we respond to this challenge.

The fact is, America is not broken. It's Washington, D.C., that's broken. The Founders gave us the ability to do something about it.

I know we can.

Eight

The Fix

*The people have an indubitable, unalienable, and indefeasible
right to reform or change their Government, whenever it be found
adverse or inadequate to the purposes of its institution.*

—James Madison, 1789

Dr. Tony Evans, a pastor in Texas, tells a story about a man with an
old house.

The walls in the house were cracked, and the owner wanted them
fixed. He called a contractor who came out and patched the cracks
and painted the walls. The house looked as good as new, and the
homeowner was pleased.

The next year, the cracks began to reappear. The man once again
called the contractor, who once again came to the house and fixed the
cracks and painted the walls.

After another year passed, the cracks reappeared *again*. By this
time the homeowner was frustrated. He angrily called the contractor
and said, "Listen, I already paid you twice to fix these cracks, but
they keep coming back!"

"Well," the builder replied, "I can patch and paint the cracks all you want. But the cracks will always reappear until you fix the real problem. Your real problem is your foundation. Until you fix your foundation, the problems will never go away."

PATCHING AND PAINTING

This is an appropriate metaphor for how our government functions today. Each branch of government bustles around creating pages of legal wallpaper, trying to cover up the endless number of cracks. They sure look busy. But in reality, nothing's accomplished.

All the while, the *cause* of the cracks is never addressed, and our country becomes even more damaged. The real problem causing the cracks in our nation's walls is that we have abandoned the solid foundation intended by our architects—the Founders—and have erected new government schemes that depart from the Constitution.

Until America addresses the core problem by repairing the foundation, the cracks will continue to surface.

This problem is particularly notable at election time. Politicians are the equivalent of contractors going door-to-door promising house repairs, but never really doing anything to fix the real problem—the foundation.

Too many Americans are sucked into this scheme. They want a quick fix for pressing problems. They elect the person who promises the best fix, in the hope that *this time* real improvements will come.

The problem with that hope is that no person alone can fix the problems that ail our nation because whoever is elected inherits a system built on a faulty foundation.

When we pin our hopes on a person, an election, a policy, or a law, we're doing what the homeowner was doing. These strategies can make things look better, but only for a while. If we want to fix the problems we face today, we need to repair the fractured foundation of our government.

GROUNDWORK

So how do we fix the foundation? How do we restore the rule of law in this nation and clamp down on the arbitrary "rule of men" that the Founders sought to prevent? How do we return our government to its constitutional moorings? The answer is surprisingly simple.

We do what the architects of the Constitution expected us to do, and what they empowered us to do—what the Founders themselves did.

After the Constitution was passed in 1787, the Founders and other critics immediately demanded that amendments be added to fix problems in the document they had just passed.[1]

Supreme Court justice Joseph Story, one of the earliest and most storied (pun intended) justices, explained: The Constitution's "framers were not bold or rash enough to believe . . . it to be perfect." Instead, "they knew, that time might develop many defects in its arrangements, and many deficiencies in its powers. They desired, that it might be open to improvement."[2]

During Congress's first session, in 1789, they set out to improve the Constitution by amending it. Just as today there is much hand-wringing about whether the Constitution should be amended, the same was true in 1789. But after contentious arguments for and against amending it, the first session of Congress eventually agreed on twelve amendments to the Constitution.

Only ten of those amendments were ratified by the states at the time. They became known as the Bill of Rights, the first ten amendments to the Constitution.[3]

To amend the Constitution, the first Congress used Article V of the Constitution. It is the same provision that has been used for each of the amendments to the Constitution.

Article V reads as follows:

> *The Congress*, whenever two thirds of both Houses shall deem it necessary, shall propose Amendments to this Constitution, or, *on the Application of the Legislatures of two thirds of the several States, shall call a Convention for proposing Amendments*, which, in either Case, shall be valid to all Intents and Purposes, as Part of this Constitution, when ratified by the Legislatures of three fourths of the several States, or by Conventions in three fourths thereof, as the one or the other Mode of Ratification may be proposed by the Congress; Provided that no Amendment which may be made prior to the Year One thousand eight hundred and eight shall in any Manner affect the first and fourth Clauses in the Ninth Section of the first Article; and that no State, without its Consent, shall be deprived of its equal Suffrage in the Senate.

To summarize, Article V provides two ways to amend the Constitution. One is for Congress to propose constitutional amendments by a two-thirds vote in both the House and Senate.

The second way is the highlighted section in Article V above. It authorizes two-thirds of state legislatures to call for a convention where constitutional amendments are proposed and voted on. This path gives states and citizens a greater say in the amendment process. Empowering states to amend the Constitution is a superior way to protect states against federal overreach.[4]

Under each path to amending the Constitution, no amendment becomes effective until it's ratified by three-fourths of the states. It takes thirty-four states to call for amendments, and it takes thirty-eight states to ratify—or pass—an amendment.

STATES CAN FIX THE FOUNDATION

America can no longer count on Congress to take the first path to amend the Constitution. Congress is part of the problem.

The cure to the frequent departures from constitutional principles by all three branches of government will not come from Washington, D.C. Instead, the states must lead the way.

If you're like me, you may be a little apprehensive about states taking on the task of proposing constitutional amendments. I've seen calls for this type of action for years, but never gave it much thought because I was more accustomed to Congress proposing amendments.

But the more I fought Washington, the more I realized the necessity of restoring America to the rule of law. So I decided to dig deep into the pros and cons of the states leading the way. What I've learned is that the *facts* behind states leading the Article V process erode the *fears* raised about states proposing amendments.

First, understand that having concerns about amending the Constitution is natural and not unexpected. Even in 1789, there was substantial concern and endless debate across the young country about whether to amend the Constitution to include the Bill of Rights: concerns that it would open the country up to having the Constitution rewritten, and questions about whether the amendments would go too far—or not far enough.

Still others argued that amendments weren't needed at all.[5] They believed that the Constitution was just fine the way it was.

Sound familiar? Seems like some things never change. Many people today express the same concerns about states leading the way to amend the Constitution, just as citizens expressed concern about the Founders amending the Constitution.

But think how America would be if Madison and others had given in to those concerns and just dropped the issue of amending the Constitution. If the naysayers had prevailed, the Bill of Rights would not have been added.

We face the same consequence today. Just like Madison, Americans who want to ensure the Constitution protects states and individuals from federal overreach face pushback from naysayers who fear altering the status quo.

Rather than letting concerns paralyze you, let your dedication to our country drive you to take action and help America restore the rule of law.

Some contend that allowing states, rather than Congress, to lead the amendment process is a radical departure from the Constitution. To the contrary, it is expressly established in the Constitution—you saw it with your own eyes in Article V. Additionally, a state-led amendment process is exactly what the Founders expected to thwart an overreaching federal government. The Founders specifically wanted you and your state legislators to have the ability to amend the Constitution as needed.

Congress can't be counted on to curb federal power. There come times in this country when the people themselves need to lead. Now is one of those times.

Moreover, a state-led process to amend the Constitution is not a new idea. It is an approach that has been sought many times. In

1977, Texas joined other states to call for a convention of states to propose a balanced budget amendment. At one time, the balanced budget amendment proposal was only two states short of the thirty-four needed to call a convention on the issue.[6]

Similarly, a state-led effort to limit income tax rates was, at one time, only two states short of going into effect.[7]

A push by the states to call a convention for the direct election of U.S. senators was only one state short of the two-thirds needed when Congress preempted the effort by proposing the amendment itself.[8]

PROFOUND AND POSITIVE

Another concern expressed by some people is that they like the Constitution just as it is and believe it shouldn't ever be changed. That's fine, but it contradicts both what the Founders intended and what they did. It also contradicts American history. (Coincidentally, many of these naysayers happen to benefit from the status quo. Follow the money and follow the power.)

Contrary to the naysayers, the Founders expressly intended the Constitution to be amended. That's why they inserted Article V. And, just as the Founders predicted, history has revealed that flaws did in fact exist in the Constitution's original design.

For example, the Thirteenth Amendment abolished slavery.

The Fifteenth Amendment ensured that citizens can't be denied the right to vote on the basis of their race, color, or prior slavery.

The Nineteenth Amendment guaranteed women the right to vote.

The Twenty-Fourth Amendment abolished the poll tax.

None of these profound changes to the Constitution, and our society, would have occurred without constitutional amendments, and without overcoming the arguments of the naysayers.

Several amendments to the Constitution deal with elections. The Seventeenth Amendment changed the way senators are selected, and the Twelfth Amendment modified the process for electing the president and vice president. The Twelfth Amendment was later modified further by the Twentieth Amendment.

The Constitution has been amended to adjust for the attitudes of the day. For example, the Eighteenth Amendment prohibited the manufacture, transportation, or sale of alcohol. The Twenty-First Amendment prohibited the prohibition by repealing the Eighteenth Amendment.

The Sixteenth Amendment empowered Congress to impose an income tax. Might the people one day follow the path of the Twenty-First Amendment and use another amendment to repeal the Sixteenth?

History has shown that the Constitution can and should be amended. History has also revealed that profound amendments occurred only when the will of the people was galvanized.

RUNAWAY CONVENTIONS

The most common concern raised about a convention of states to amend the Constitution under Article V is the unfounded fear of a "runaway" convention. There are several reasons why this simply would not happen.

One is math.

At least *thirty-four* states must agree to even hold a convention to consider proposed constitutional amendments. That means that just seventeen states can block a convention of states from even occurring if it appears the convention could run out of control. That daunting mathematical hurdle should weed out any proposals that could somehow be characterized as radical.

From there, the math gets even tougher. Any proposal that survives the thirty-four-state convention gauntlet still must be agreed upon by thirty-eight states before the proposal can be ratified. That means that just thirteen states can block any proposal from becoming an amendment to the Constitution.

When you realize that it requires only thirteen states to block a "runaway" convention, you'll also understand that anyone who fears a runaway convention must be using Common Core math.

A wholesale rewrite of the Constitution, or other extreme proposals, will be unacceptable to at least the thirteen states needed to block it.

But, for those still concerned, there are additional safeguards. States can limit the topics for discussion at the convention itself. For example, five of the current states that have called for a convention of states have limited their proposal to specific issues.[9]

Additionally, any state legislature that agrees to a convention of states can limit the issues their state can vote on. State legislatures can even mandate a "no" vote against any provision not authorized in advance or even dissolve the state's consent to participate if the convention strays from the originally proposed topics.

As one example, to thwart a convention of states from rewriting the entire Constitution rather than remaining limited to several proposed amendments, states can—in advance—require their delegations to vote against such a sweeping proposal or withdraw from the convention itself.

Another limitation is time. State legislatures that authorize amendments, and a convention of states that passes amendments, can put time limits on the ratification of amendments. For example, the Twenty-Second Amendment provides that the amendment would be "inoperative" unless it is ratified by three-fourths of the states within seven years.

The guardrails preventing a runaway convention are many.

I KNOW WE CAN

Lastly, many naysayers argue that trying to amend the Constitution is a waste of time because it's too hard to do. To the contrary, all it takes is one person with backbone. It could be you.

In 1982, as a sophomore at my alma mater the University of Texas, Gregory Watson was preparing a research paper for a government class. While searching for a topic for his paper, Watson stumbled upon an amendment that Congress had passed but which had not been ratified by the United States.

Watson was fascinated with the proposed amendment and wrote his paper on how it could be ratified and urged its adoption. His teacher was unimpressed and gave him a C.

Undeterred, Watson persisted. By now this issue was far larger to Watson than any paper or any grade. It was a cause. He took upon himself the cause to try to get the amendment ratified.

Watson began a letter-writing campaign to state legislatures across the country requesting states ratify the proposed amendment. This was long before Twitter and Facebook.

The challenge was daunting for one monumental reason. Congress passed the proposed amendment in *1789*, almost two hundred years before Watson wrote his research paper.

There was another immovable obstacle. Law professors, politicians, and pundits agreed that there was no chance to resurrect a proposed constitutional amendment that was almost two centuries old.

But Watson was no law professor, politician, or pundit. He was an American citizen. Watson pressed on.

By now, he had captured the attention of a force more powerful than the established class. He had gained the support of the people of the United States.

A big reason was the subject of the amendment: congressional pay. In the midst of public backlash against Congress in the 1980s, Watson latched on to a topic that resonated with the people.

As congressional salaries increased, and as Congress's power expanded, public anger with Congress exploded. The public was all too eager to pass a law that Congress wouldn't pass itself: a law reining in Congress.

As proposed by James Madison in 1789, the amendment read:

> No law, varying the compensation for the services of the Senators and Representatives, shall take effect, until an election of Representatives shall have intervened.

Unlike what became the Bill of Rights, Madison's amendment to congressional pay never received enough votes to be ratified. By 1791 only six states had ratified the amendment. So it largely languished for the better part of two centuries.

Between the time Madison left the amendment and Watson picked it up, three more states had ratified it.

Slowly but surely, Watson was able to get one state, then another, to ratify the amendment. First it was Maine, then Colorado. Ten, then twenty, then thirty-seven states ratified it. On May 7, 1992, Michigan became the thirty-eighth state to ratify the amendment.

The naysayers were wrong because they didn't understand the effect that a single person with backbone can have in our country.

Watson's college research paper for which he received a C turned into the Twenty-Seventh Amendment to the Constitution.

One person can make a difference.[10]

RIGHT TO REFORM

James Madison, the Constitution's primary architect, stated in 1789—two years after the Constitution passed—that the people have an "indubitable, unalienable, and indefeasible right to reform or change their government, whenever it be found adverse or inadequate to the purposes of its institution."[11] He then began amending the Constitution.

I'll take Madison's advice over those who argue that we can't, or shouldn't, do anything to mend the Constitution.

We've felt the weight of oppressive laws passed by Congress, we've watched the president create "laws" with a pen and a phone, and we've witnessed courts rewrite the Constitution itself. Power is shifting to Washington, D.C., and away from you and your neighbors. We've sent countless elected officials to fight problems, only to see those officials become part of the problem.

I believe we're beyond the question of *whether* we need to amend the Constitution. Clearly this document, the foundation for every law in this country, is being disregarded by all three branches of government.

Instead, the only question is *how* we amend it.

That's an issue for your state to decide. States must first agree to modify the Constitution, as have states like Florida, Tennessee, Alabama, Georgia, and Alaska. Dozens of other states are actively working toward it.

It's an issue that you must help decide.

I have concrete proposals to fix our nation's crumbling foundation and restore the rule of law. The ideas in the following chapters are not theoretical proposals developed by some think tank or pundit-philosopher. Instead, each proposal comes from lessons learned in my battles for the Constitution.

What you and I know for certain is what doesn't work. The status quo doesn't work.

My proposals are based on fights I've waged throughout my career.

Before I took the bar exam, I studied. And studied. I was scared but prepared. And I passed on my first attempt.

When taking on a legal challenge in private practice, I did my homework, answered objections, and entered the courtroom prepared to win.

As a judge on the Texas Supreme Court, I was ready when the bailiff announced my entry. I'd thoroughly reviewed both sides of the case, and past cases.

I faced federal Goliaths in courts across the nation as Texas attorney general, including the United States Supreme Court, where we won the support of other states, and won landmark decisions.

As governor, I've marshaled the strongest border security effort of any state—ever—to combat the federal government's failure to do its job, I've cut taxes when other states were raising them, and I expanded Second Amendment rights in the face of federal threats to rein them in.

Here's the point: when it comes to tough challenges, I have a history of preparing, building consensus, and winning. We've won "impossible" fights when others ran from the battle.

Some politicians talk about having a spine of steel. I actually have one. And I've used my steel spine to fight for liberty against an overreaching federal government.

YES. SERIOUSLY.

Every time Americans have faced a challenge, they were up to that challenge. Now must be no different.

Slowly but surely, our citizens have been fooled into believing that we just need the right person or policy to fix the country. In reality, we've merely been arguing about patches and paint.

Our challenge is to fix the foundation rather than continue the current practice of patching over our problems with temporary fixes that often do more harm than good. We need to force our lawmakers to return to the rule of law.

We can do this.

If you don't think so, just ask the guy who became paralyzed in 1984, and went on to become governor.

Ask Gregory Watson, who got the Twenty-Seventh Amendment passed.

Ask every woman or racial minority who votes if the difficulty of amending the Constitution was worth the effort.

When you think about it, even our Declaration of Independence was viewed as impossible and naïve by many, and yet a few people who pledged their lives, fortunes, and sacred honor were able to make a difference that changed the world.

Let's get our eyes off political candidates for a minute. They are not the answer to our problems. Instead, let's focus on solutions, and our role in implementing them.

You Are the Answer

Our broken government will be fixed only if you are engaged. The monumental movements that created and elevated this nation were carried by one group: the people of America. You and other readers of this book are the coauthors of the future of this nation.

America's destiny is in your hands. If you sit on the sidelines and don't get into the game, the United States of America will continue to crumble.

If you agree it's time to restore our foundation—if you have the guts Americans have displayed throughout the history of our nation and take action—you will help create a brighter future for America.

The Constitution was written with one person in mind: you, the American citizen.

But over time, the United States has begun to repeat the sobering history of fallen nations as political leaders and bureaucrats amass power to themselves. Remember the economic collapse of 2008 and 2009, when your property values decreased, your retirement fund vaporized, and your job was threatened? I do.

Remember how Congress cut their pay, and how government agencies trimmed regulations, and their workforces, to help cut the deficit? Me neither. Instead, federal politicians exploded spending, imposed onerous regulations on employers and individuals, and have seized upon every fear to control your lives even more.

Think about this. "Gross Domestic Product is the single best indicator of economic health. Since 1947, U.S. GDP, the sum of all goods and services produced, has risen at an average rate of 3.3%. But since 2001, the average rate has been just 1.9%. The last time GDP grew more than 3% was in 2005." And the U.S. labor participation rate has fallen to the lowest since the U.S. economic malaise under President Jimmy Carter.[12]

How can this be? I submit, based on employers I talk with, that it's because of all those new regulations and the costs they impose on starting and growing a business. Employers and employees (and potential hires) are hurt by these regulations.

If we don't fight, the person who gets left out of this is you.

Many Americans have been so beaten down by the governmental status quo that they've lost hope for real change. Despite election-year promises, there is no one person who can be a rescue agent, because that person will inherit a cracked system.

As I said earlier, I've sued the federal government thirty-four times. I filed those lawsuits because we have a government that defies the Constitution. These efforts were, and are still, necessary. But I was just repairing the cracks.

Whoever moves into the White House, the Capitol Building, or the Supreme Court Building will find cracks in the walls—until the foundation of all of them is fixed.

Only *we* can fix that foundation.

Nine

Teeth in the Tenth

The powers delegated by the proposed Constitution to the federal
government, are few and defined. Those which are to remain
in the State governments are numerous and indefinite.
—JAMES MADISON, *FEDERALIST* 45, JANUARY 1788

Status quo is a Latin term meaning "just another dysfunctional day in Washington, D.C."

Maybe that's not the exact definition, but one thing we can probably agree on is that the federal power-grabbing of Washington, D.C., is both dysfunctional for our country and inconsistent with our constitutional design.

One solution to the problem is to fight against Washington, which I've done as attorney general and governor. But if the status quo doesn't change, we'll be fighting for generations, while we watch more of our freedom slip away.

Conventional wisdom, especially at political conventions, is that we can fix a broken government by electing the right people.

Sounds perfect. But how many decades have we been trying

this solution? And how many officials have disappointed us as they became part of the system they were elected to change?

As much as I, and others, like to sue Barack Obama, he's not the only problem. The problem is far bigger than any one person.

Our country got off track decades ago, most profoundly during the Roosevelt administration. FDR's "New Deal" turned out to be a raw deal for the Constitution. At the time, the country's economy was in deep trouble, so people were okay with a few rewrites of the Constitution and some increases in federal power—even though those modifications didn't go through the Article V amendment process. After all, it was for our own good!

Sound familiar?

It's simply the nature of the system to perpetuate the system. As Ronald Reagan said, "The nearest thing to eternal life we will ever see on this earth is a government program."

The root problems that face our country will not be fixed just by fighting, or complaining, or by simply changing the names of our leaders. We must fix our foundation by steering the country back on the path of the Constitution.

A COUNTRY POWERED BY STATES

Unlike many nations, America was not established by conquerors. Instead it was created by defenders of liberty.

The Founders didn't fight so that government could tax more, regulate more, and put you deeper in debt. Instead they fought against Great Britain for one word: *freedom*.

The architects of the Constitution knew that in America the

ruling class was not kings or conquerors; instead it was the people themselves.

Part of the genius of the Constitution is that it's not a dictate from a centralized government, it's a document where people—through the states—give limited power to their federal government.

As a result, the *real* power in America is designed to remain with the people. That's why the United States, more than any other country, is the place where a person can chart their own course to achieve their dreams.

After passing the Constitution in 1787, the Founders knew that the rights of individuals, and the state governments closest to them, must be safeguarded from future threats. They knew from history about the capability, if not the probability, that rulers are inclined to expand their power at the expense of the people. So they built a bulwark against that threat by passing the first ten amendments to the Constitution—also known as the Bill of Rights.

You're familiar with amendments that protect individual liberties. The First Amendment protects your freedom of religion and free speech. The Second Amendment protects the right of the people to keep and bear arms.

There's also an amendment that cements into the Constitution America's original design: we are a country created by states and the people, and true authority lies with them. It's the Tenth Amendment.

The Tenth Amendment reads:

> The powers not delegated to the United States by the Constitution, nor prohibited by it to the States, are reserved to the States respectively, or to the people.

That's simple and straightforward. All power in this country is reserved for the states and the people, except for the powers they delegated to the United States in the Constitution itself.

The truth of the matter is the states held all the power at the founding of this country and they gave a few powers to the federal government—not the other way around.

James Madison wrote essays about the Constitution's intent. One of them, *Federalist* 45, foreshadowed the Tenth Amendment.

I think you'll be amazed by the clarity of what he wrote. (I think you'll also be disturbed by how far the country has strayed from Madison's original guidance.) Here's an excerpt:

> The powers delegated by the proposed Constitution to the federal government, are few and defined. Those which are to remain in the State governments are numerous and indefinite.
>
> The former will be exercised principally on external objects, as war, peace, negotiation, and foreign commerce; with which last the power of taxation will, for the most part, be connected.
>
> The powers reserved to the several States will extend to all the objects which, in the ordinary course of affairs, concern the lives, liberties, and properties of the people, and the internal order, improvement, and prosperity of the State.

Madison was crystal clear: the federal government was purposefully designed to be limited. And he was quite specific that the Constitution intended that states—not the federal government—govern matters concerning life, liberty, and the property of the people.

The Tenth Amendment gives the states a check and balance against the federal government to prevent it from gaining the type of power England had over the colonies—a brilliant solution.

SO, WHAT HAPPENED?

If I've heard it once, I've heard it a thousand times: "Just enforce the Tenth Amendment."

When illegal immigrants cross the border, people ask: "Why don't you just enforce the Tenth Amendment?"

When Barack Obama issues a dubious executive order, I get the same question: "Why don't you just enforce the Tenth Amendment?"

That's a common rallying cry of citizens frustrated with our federal government. It's eerily similar to the colonists' complaint about a distant government that ran too much of their lives, spent too much of their money, and failed to solve their real challenges.

The Tenth Amendment was supposed to protect against federal power grabs. What happened?

The problem with enforcing the Tenth Amendment is twofold. First, all three branches of government have emasculated the Tenth Amendment as a way to consolidate power in Washington and to weaken state autonomy and authority. They simply ignore the power that was intended to remain in the states.

Second, there is no enforcement component to the Tenth Amendment. Because the amendment does not include a clear consequence, or remedy, for violating it, judges often refuse to enforce it. Even when state sovereignty is overtly violated, courts deny states, and individuals in those states, the authority to challenge the violation. Courts have increasingly concluded that the federal government can regulate in areas that were reserved to the states.

The cement that formed the foundation of our country, the bond that secured our constitutional structure that protected states and individuals, was instilled in the Tenth Amendment.

For more than a century, the Supreme Court had nipped and tucked around the edges of the Tenth Amendment. Limiting it here, contracting it there, but nothing drastic all at once. Slowly but surely, rulings modified the amendment's original intent in ways that didn't raise the hackles of the states.

In the legal universe, past court decisions always influence future cases, and often dictate how judges will decide. As more and more abuses of the Tenth Amendment piled up, these *precedents* eventually tipped the scales of justice until they were broken.

DEVOURING THE STATES

The Tenth Amendment had one last gasp before being demolished.

In a 5–4 decision in 1976, the Supreme Court upheld the Tenth Amendment's intended purpose in *National League of Cities v. Usery.*

The case involved whether the federal government can dictate to state and local governments how much they pay their employees.

Let's remember what Madison said about the principles that underlie the Tenth Amendment, and the division of power between state and federal governments:

> The powers delegated by the proposed Constitution to the federal government, are few and defined. Those which are to remain in the State governments are numerous and indefinite.
>
> The powers reserved to the several States will extend to all the objects which, in the ordinary course of affairs, concern the lives, liberties, and properties of the people, and the internal order, improvement, and prosperity of the State.

This issue should be a no-brainer, right? Clearly under Madison's explanation, state and local governments should determine how much they pay their employees. I can assure you that you won't find a single sentence in the Constitution where the states delegated that authority to the federal government.

In *National League of Cities*, the Supreme Court agreed. The Court concluded that "decisions by a State concerning the wages and hours of its employees are an 'undoubted attribute of state sovereignty.'"

Of note, Justice Harry Blackmun concurred in the decision. That means that he agreed with its outcome, but wrote his own opinion.

The central theme of the Court's decision echoed what Madison articulated: "The States occupy a special position in our constitutional system, and the scope of Congress' authority must reflect that position."

A later Supreme Court decision explained: *National League of Cities* reflected the general conviction that the Constitution precluded "the National Government [from] devour[ing] the essentials of state sovereignty."

But less than a decade later, the power of the Tenth Amendment was dealt a massive blow—almost as if a huge tree had fallen on it.

In a 5–4 decision in 1985, the Supreme Court issued *Garcia v. San Antonio Metropolitan Transit Authority*. The Court reconsidered the very same law at issue in *National League of Cities* and overruled that earlier decision.

This time, the Court ruled that the federal government *can* dictate how much a local government agency must pay its employees. Directly contrary to *National League of Cities*, the Court in *Garcia* said that nothing in the federal law regulating how the local government pays employees "is destructive of state sovereignty or violative of any constitutional provision."

In the nine years between 1976 and 1985, the Constitution hadn't changed. What changed was Justice Blackmun's opinion about the Constitution. He switched sides and wrote the opinion that effectively rewrote the Tenth Amendment.

In *Garcia*, the Court rejected "as unsound in principle and unworkable in practice a rule of state immunity from federal regulation that turns on a judicial appraisal." By this the Court was saying that it was no longer going to play a role in determining whether the Tenth Amendment protects states from an overreaching federal government.

An even shorter translation could read: The Tenth Amendment shouldn't be reviewed by courts.

The Court gave an astonishing reason. The majority opinion stated:

> Federal Government was designed in large part to protect the States from overreaching by Congress. The Framers thus gave the States a role in the selection both of the Executive and the Legislative Branches of the Federal Government. The States were vested with indirect influence over the House of Representatives and the Presidency by their control of electoral qualifications and their role in Presidential elections. U.S. Const., Art. I, § 2, and Art. II, § 1. They were given more direct influence in the Senate, where each State received equal representation and each Senator was to be selected by the legislature of his State.
>
> [T]he Framers chose to rely on a federal system in which special restraints on federal power over the States inhered prin-

cipally in the workings of the National Government itself, rather than in discrete limitations on the objects of federal authority. State sovereign interests, then, are more properly protected by procedural safeguards inherent in the structure of the federal system than by judicially created limitations on federal power.

What does this mean? The Court explained: "The political process ensures that laws that unduly burden the States will not be promulgated."

The Supreme Court here, as it has done so often, simply fabricated a supposed constitutional principle out of thin air. Nothing in the Constitution or its history supports this bizarre conclusion. To the contrary, the Constitution *does* have the Tenth Amendment, which dictates that "laws that unduly burden the States will not be promulgated."

That Court's false presumption that the political process rather than the rule of law would protect the states had to be the height of naïveté. Or worse, just a poor excuse for rewriting the Constitution.

The Supreme Court claimed that it would be too "difficult" for judges to decide if a federal law infringes on the Tenth Amendment. So, instead, the Court ruled that states and individuals must protect themselves by electing the officials in Washington, D.C., who will protect Tenth Amendment rights.

The Supreme Court literally ruled that elections, not the Tenth Amendment, will protect states and individuals from the federal government.

That's absurd!

The Tenth Amendment, which Madison intended to protect states and individuals from the federal government, is now dependent on *federal leaders* to protect states. The Supreme Court's ruling did more than turn the Tenth Amendment on its head. It took a sledgehammer to the foundation of the Constitution.

Does the Court really believe that voters in Maine or Oregon can protect against outlandish congressional behavior like the Cornhusker Kickback? Or that voters in Kentucky will be able to protect against federal ineptitude about securing the border?

The dissenting opinion in *Garcia* rightly pointed out that the majority decision "substantially alters the federal system embodied in the Constitution." It sums up the situation:

> A unique feature of the United States is the federal system of government guaranteed by the Constitution and implicit in the very name of our country. Despite some genuflecting in the Court's opinion to the concept of federalism, today's decision effectively reduces the Tenth Amendment to meaningless rhetoric.[1]

The citizens who adamantly demand that the state enforce the Tenth Amendment have no idea of the extent to which courts have ruled that the amendment no longer protects citizens and states from an overreaching federal government.

But that didn't stop us from trying.

KNOCKED DOWN BUT NOT KNOCKED OUT

My thirty-first lawsuit against the Obama administration, which halted President Obama's executive order granting amnesty to millions of people in America illegally, was not the first lawsuit Texas waged about a broken immigration system.

In August 1994, eight years before I became attorney general, Texas sued the federal government in the same Brownsville court where my thirty-first lawsuit was filed.

The lawsuit alleged "that hundreds of thousands of undocumented immigrants live in Texas as the direct consequence of federal immigration policy." It contended that the federal government "violated the Constitution and immigration laws by failing to control illegal immigration and by failing to reimburse Texas for its educational, medical, and criminal justice expenditures on undocumented aliens." Those expenditures were about $1.34 billion for 1993 alone.

Our allegations included violations of the Tenth Amendment. Nine years after the Supreme Court drove a stake through the heart of the Tenth Amendment, Texas tried to resurrect it.

The trial court dismissed Texas's claims and the state appealed to the United States Court of Appeals for the Fifth Circuit. The Court of Appeals issued its decision on February 28, 1997.

It took just one page to dispatch with the Tenth Amendment claims. The court wrote: "The State's correctional expenses stem from its enforcement of its own penal laws, not federal laws."

Well, yeah.

It seemed irrelevant to the court that the penal action Texas took was for one reason: the federal government had failed to do its job to secure the border and impose effective immigration laws.

In other words, the states were left on the hook because of federal government malfeasance. I'm no psychologist, but this seems like classic passive-aggressive behavior. But wait! It gets worse.

In the same sentence, the court continued: "and federal law requires states to provide emergency medical care to undocumented aliens only if the states voluntarily choose to receive federal funds from the Medicaid program."

So the court forced Texas into an untenable choice: we must provide health care to people here illegally or risk losing billions in Medicaid funding to care for American citizens.

That's precisely the heavy hand of government that Madison intended the Tenth Amendment to protect against.

The court added, "Finally, the State's public education expenditures for the children of undocumented aliens are required by the equal protection clause rather than by actions of the federal defendants." That conclusion was dictated by the *Plyler v. Doe* Supreme Court decision in 1982.

This is another Alice in Wonderland ruling. Because a federal branch of government (the judiciary) ruled that states are required to provide education for people in our state illegally, the state can't recover from the federal government costs incurred because the federal government isn't doing its job.

If you think reading that paragraph is hard, welcome to my world!

Concluding that Texas's lawsuit "raises questions of policy rather than colorable claims of constitutional or statutory violations," the Court of Appeals agreed with the trial court decision to dismiss our case.

The court's ruling meant that the Texas state budget—and hence Texas taxpayers—were compelled to pay for the federal government's failure to control illegal immigration. The states truly had become the servants of the federal government—the very situation the Founders feared. They inserted the Tenth Amendment in the Bill of Rights to protect against this very type of "usurpation."

Left: From my days in Little League.
AUTHOR'S COLLECTION

Above: Running track in high school.
AUTHOR'S COLLECTION

Above: Graduating from Duncanville High School.
AUTHOR'S COLLECTION

Above: Graduating from Vanderbilt Law School.
AUTHOR'S COLLECTION

Left: Marrying Cecilia.
AUTHOR'S COLLECTION

Right: Recovering at the hospital in a
body jacket, aka the "turtle shell."
AUTHOR'S COLLECTION

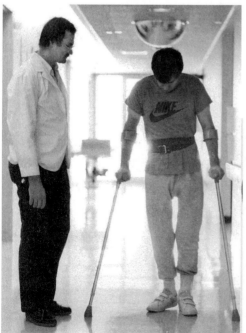

Right and Above: In rehabilitation after my accident.
AUTHOR'S COLLECTION

Left: With my mother outside the rehab center.
AUTHOR'S COLLECTION

Above: Being sworn in as State District Judge, with my mother in the foreground.
AUTHOR'S COLLECTION

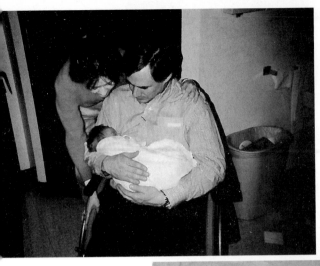

Left: The first time I held Audrey after she was born.
AUTHOR'S COLLECTION

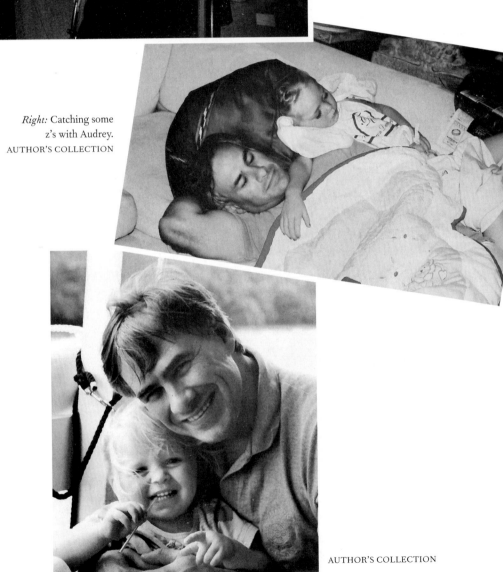

Right: Catching some z's with Audrey.
AUTHOR'S COLLECTION

AUTHOR'S COLLECTION

Left: On Texas Capitol Grounds with the Ten Commandments display I defended at the United States Supreme Court. TEXAS ATTORNEY GENERAL'S OFFICE

Above: With Ted Cruz, who served as solicitor general when I was attorney general. TEXANS FOR GREG ABBOTT

Left: At a function with Cecilia. AUTHOR'S COLLECTION

Left: Discussing my plan for a convention of states at the Texas Public Policy Foundation.
OFFICE OF THE GOVERNOR

Right: Honoring veterans and posthumously awarding the Texas Legislative Medal of Honor to Chief Petty Officer Chris Kyle and Lieutenant Colonel Ed Dyess.
OFFICE OF THE GOVERNOR

Left: Discussing lawsuit to protect religious liberties of Kountze High School cheerleaders.
TEXAS ATTORNEY GENERAL'S OFFICE

Above: Being sworn in as Texas's forty-eighth governor.
OFFICE OF THE GOVERNOR

Right: Discussing
Texas's lawsuit against
President Obama's
executive amnesty
action.
TEXAS ATTORNEY
GENERAL'S OFFICE

Left: Meeting with
President Obama in Oval
Office after being elected
governor.
BRENDAN SMIALOWSKI /
GETTY IMAGES

By the time the Fifth Circuit had rejected our claims, the Supreme Court had already rejected similar claims asserted by Arizona, California, Florida, New Jersey, and New York. That made an appeal of the Fifth Circuit ruling impossible.

Before leaving this case, I have to share what the Court of Appeals wrote in its last paragraph: "We reject out-of-hand the State's contention that the federal defendants' alleged systemic failure to control immigration is so extreme as to constitute a reviewable abdication of duty."

That fallacy was proven wrong two decades later when a federal judge in Brownsville wrote that the federal government was a "co-conspirator" in allowing our immigrations laws to be broken.

Finally, a judge with backbone.

TIP OF THE ICEBERG

These cases are the tip of the iceberg lurking under our waters. They are just a sampling of the ways our federal government has trampled on states—on your freedom! Over the past century we've experienced the relentless march of government intruding into the affairs that Madison insisted would be left to the states.

Remember this quote?

> The powers reserved to the several States will extend to all the objects which, in the ordinary course of affairs, concern the lives, liberties, and properties of the people.

It seems almost quaint now.

The expansion of federal law preemption shows just how diminished states have become in their ability to influence the lives of their citizens.

State power is evaporating over activities like driver's licenses, labor and employment practices, occupational health and safety, and even habeas corpus and meat inspection. Those last two are especially disturbing because under our constitutional architecture, states are given the power to supervise their criminal justice systems and to exercise police powers like inspecting slaughterhouses.

Almost a century ago, Supreme Court justice Louis Brandeis wrote: "It is one of the happy incidents of the federal system that a single courageous state may, if its citizens choose, serve as a laboratory; and try novel social and economic experiments without risk to the rest of the country." [2]

This ideal allows citizens to vote with their feet. They can move to the state that best represents their social and economic views.

Texas has been on the receiving end of this dynamic. Over the past decade—and over the past year—more people have moved to Texas than any other state. They must like it here, or found a job here, or both!

If they change their mind, they can move to another state that fits them better, while still enjoying the fruits that come from our federal constitutional structure.

But the freedom to choose, this framework that compels states to compete with each other, is eliminated with the increasing one-size-fits-all preemptive law from the federal level.

I Have an App for That

In the tech world, Apple created what became a ubiquitous catchphrase, "There's an app for that."

The slogan helped Apple hammer home the idea that if you had a need, they had the solution. At last count, the App Store had well over 250,000 apps, or applications, for their devices. Apple even got a trademark for the phrase.

I just checked both my laptop and cell phone and found no app for "constitutional amendment." I couldn't find one for "fixing a broken constitution," either.

So I'm going to provide my own apps, or fixes, for what ails the Tenth Amendment. States should consider supporting these solutions at a convention of states like what I discussed in the previous chapter.

One solution is to add *one word* to the Tenth Amendment to have it say:

> The powers not *expressly* delegated to the United States by the Constitution, nor prohibited by it to the States, are reserved to the States respectively, or to the people.

The federal government has assumed all kinds of powers that can, in any conceivable and inconceivable way, relate to authority delegated by the Constitution. That's not what was intended. That upside-down power structure is the problem.

I have a fix for that.

A lawsuit can't and won't add that one word. Justices on the Supreme Court won't add that word to the Tenth Amendment. They are the ones who took the teeth from the Tenth Amendment.

The proposed amendment would tell the federal government that it truly has only the powers specifically given to it in the Constitution, and no more. And *we really mean it this time*!

This one-word change would constrain the federal government to its intended role.

But what good is the Tenth Amendment if it can't be enforced? We can no longer allow courts to bob and weave away from their obligation to enforce the Tenth Amendment.

I have a fix for that, too!

Some amendments have multiple sections. The Fourteenth Amendment, for example, has five sections. The Twentieth Amendment has six sections.

I propose adding one more section to the Tenth Amendment, one that gives states the authority to enforce the Tenth Amendment against the federal government if it exceeds its enumerated powers. Without enforcement, an amendment has no teeth.

We've seen how the federal government has exceeded its enumerated powers, how it has violated the Constitution, how it has denigrated the states' authority, all the while making states less powerful to stop it.

With this added section to the Tenth Amendment, courts, as in the *Garcia* case and the *Texas v. U.S.* case discussed above, can no longer hide behind their fabricated idea that it's too complicated to enforce the Tenth Amendment, or that Tenth Amendment issues must be resolved at the ballot box.

Instead, just as Madison and his coauthors intended, the federal government will be limited only to the powers given it in the Constitution. The remaining powers will be with the people and the states. If the federal government strays beyond that line, states will have the power to rein it in.

The rule of law requires that *someone* have the power to keep the federal government in line. The states are the proper party to play that role.

That's the way our country was intended to work. It's called accountability. Washington, D.C., needs more of it.

Ten

Secret Agency Law

Either you will control your government,
or government will control you.
—RONALD REAGAN

We'll start this chapter with a question. Under the Constitution, which branch of government writes the laws?

Let's see if you got it right.

Contrary to the way government is structured in many other countries, the United States was established with its citizens at the top, and public servants ranking below them.

One way this structure was built into our system is to have a president elected by the people, who can also be unelected by the people—unlike kings, or dictators, or faux democracies.

But, while you can vote for or against a presidential candidate, your vote sometimes competes with the vote of a citizen who lives a thousand miles away. That's why the president isn't authorized by the Constitution to lord over you with unbearable laws. Instead, the role of the president is confined to *enforcing* the laws, not creating them. At least in theory.

A president must answer to the people in every state. But you need someone more directly responsive to you, someone local, someone who must listen to you before they dare pass a law that tells you what to do.

That's why authority to make laws under the Constitution was given to one branch alone. The first sentence of Article I of the Constitution says:

> All legislative Powers herein granted shall be vested in a Congress of the United States, which shall consist of a Senate and House of Representatives.

The essential point is, no law affecting your life can be enacted unless it is voted on by someone you can vote to hire or fire. If your representative passes a law raising taxes, you can try to fire them with your vote. If they refuse to enact a law to help the country, you can vote for someone who will. Because your representative has an office located near where you live, you have the ability to go to that office and complain about your government and to try to influence future action by your representative.

This is the way the Constitution is supposed to work, and this is the way the Founders constructed our system of government. One problem: this is not the way things work right now.

More than 90 percent of the federal government rules and regulations that run your lives are never even voted on by Congress. Instead, most federal laws that govern America are authored by a group not even mentioned in the Constitution. This group comes from what is often referred to as the fourth branch of government—the administrative branch. The Founders would be astonished that such a powerful and unaccountable branch even exists!

Two studies from different presidential administrations show similar and startling results. In calendar year 2014, 224 acts of Congress became law, while 3,554 rules and regulations were issued by federal agencies.[1] In 2007, 138 acts of Congress became law, while 2,926 rules and regulations were issued by federal agencies.[2]

SECRET AGENTS

Who exactly are the people establishing all these rules and regulations, and what do they do?

Only the lobbyists know.

There are literally hundreds of federal agencies,[3] boards, bureaus, and commissions that run virtually every aspect of your life. They typically aren't even referenced by name, but are camouflaged by meaningless letters like: BATFE, BLM, CFPB, DHS, DOE, DOL, EEOC, EPA, FAA, FEMA, FDA, FHA, FTC, HHS, HUD, IRS, NLRB, SEC, and so on. There's probably a few others I've sued over the years. I lose track.

Contrary to the constitutional design that allows you to hire and fire the elected officials who make rules for our lives, in reality the people making those rules are unelected and unaccountable federal bureaucrats. And often, because of federal civil service rules, labor unions, and other protections, it's difficult for those bureaucrats to be fired even by the person running the agency.[4]

But it gets worse!

In addition to making all those regulations, these agencies also enforce the rules they create. And even more troublesome, they often sit in judgment whenever you, the taxpayer, dare to challenge their authority.

The average American probably believes most federal legal disputes are resolved in the courts. Not so. As with the lawmaking process, federal administrative agencies have hijacked the judicial process.

One study shows federal administrative agencies adjudicated ten times the number of cases adjudicated by federal courts.[5]

As a result, federal agencies have been described as the very prototype of "tyranny." In effect, they combine all three branches of government—legislative, executive, and judicial—into one. They make the rules, they enforce their rules, and they adjudicate them.

The Founders knew the dangers that could come from this accumulation of unaccountable power.

In *Federalist* 47, Madison warned the "accumulation of all powers, legislative, executive, and judiciary, in the same hands . . . may justly be pronounced the very definition of tyranny."

Similarly, John Adams cautioned that all three powers combined "would make arbitrary laws for their own interest, execute all laws arbitrarily for their own interest, and adjudge all controversies in their own favor."[6]

How prescient they were.

The Founders purposefully protected us from these perils by ordering the separation of powers among the legislative, executive, and judicial branches of government.

The Constitution was intended to police the roles of the *three* branches of government written into Articles I, II, and III of the document. The Constitution was not, however, structured to protect against this new fourth branch of government, because the growth of the "administrative branch" was beyond the Founders' comprehension.

To protect against government abandoning its intended role is one of the many reasons why the Founders inserted Article V into the Constitution. They wanted us to be able to respond to challenges they could not foresee; challenges to our liberty like those now imposed by administrative agencies.

How Did This Happen?

For most of our history the Constitution worked as designed. Citizens would elect representatives who would fight for their needs. Representatives would work together to pass laws based on the Constitution and the president would sign or veto them.

Over time some executive agencies were added to fulfill the constitutional mandate for the president to "take Care that the Laws be faithfully executed."

And courts played their role to keep the other two branches in check by enforcing what's called the "nondelegation doctrine." This principle prevented Congress from delegating legislative authority to the president and was viewed by the courts as vital to the integrity of the Constitution.

This nondelegation doctrine may seem obscure, but it's actually a cornerstone principle of our nation. It traces back to John Locke, who articulated the theory for giving elected officials the power to legislate and impose laws on the people. He said the legislative power is:

> a delegated Power from the People, they, who have it, cannot pass it over to others. . . . And when the people have said, We will submit to rules, and be govern'd by Laws made by such Men, and in such Forms, no Body else can say other Men shall

make Laws for them; nor can the people be bound by any Laws but such as are Enacted by those, whom they have Chosen, and Authorised to make Laws for them.[7]

In short, this means there's a compact, an agreement, between the people who entrust their power to legislators who make laws for them. This power cannot be given by those legislators to some other authority, like a bunch of unaccountable bureaucrats, because it would break that direct compact.

This agreement, involving trust and direct accountability, is the way America was constructed, and is one of the reasons we thrived as a young country.

This maxim was affirmed in 1825 by Chief Justice John Marshall, who wrote: "It will not be contended that congress can delegate to the courts, or to any other tribunals, powers which are strictly and exclusively legislative."[8]

The principle was reaffirmed through the 1800s. In 1892, the Supreme Court declared: "That Congress cannot delegate legislative power to the President is a principle universally recognized as vital to the integrity and maintenance of the system of government ordained by the constitution."[9]

As America moved into the 1900s, however, progressivism took hold, and the delegation of legislative authority began to expand. One hundred and fifty years after our nation was born, it was becoming easier to forget why the Founders fought for our freedom. It was becoming more acceptable to abandon the rigors compelled by the Constitution and, instead, alter those rules in an effort to respond to the felt needs of the day.

The original compact between the people and legislators engraved in the Constitution was becoming a distant memory.

But that compact didn't go without a fight.

In the 1930s Congress began delegating unprecedented legislative authority to the president in an effort to help him combat the Great Depression.

Congress used the National Industrial Recovery Act to give FDR authority to prohibit interstate shipment of oil if it exceeded certain quotas. This law gave the president a say in setting quotas.

In 1935, the Supreme Court ruled that Congress illegally delegated its authority under the National Industrial Recovery Act. The Supreme Court concluded that the law gave the president "functions of a Legislature rather than those of an executive or administrative officer executing a declared legislative policy." [10]

That same year, the Supreme Court also ruled that Congress overstepped its authority by delegating to the president the power to write a code regulating competition. FDR used that power to regulate the number of hours worked, the wages paid, the number of workers hired, and the collective bargaining rights of workers in chicken slaughterhouses.

The Court held that "Congress is not permitted to abdicate or to transfer to others the essential legislative functions." [11]

In short, in 1935 the Supreme Court was still denying Congress the ability to delegate its role to make laws to the administrative branch controlled by the president.

Frustrated with these adverse court rulings, FDR threatened to "pack" the Supreme Court—that is, increase the number of justices on the Court—until he was able to get rulings to his liking. [12]

Rather than having the Supreme Court expand beyond its nine justices, the Court capitulated to FDR's constitutional tinkering, and in doing so joined the president and Congress in abandoning the rule of law.

The destruction of the three branches of government was accelerated by one of FDR's top advisors, James Landis, who served in numerous positions, including on the Federal Trade Commission and as chairman of the Securities and Exchange Commission.

Landis considered the Constitution to be inconvenient. So he openly advocated to the president, Congress, and courts the necessity of altering the separation of powers among the three branches of government intended by the Founders. Instead he insisted that legislative, executive, and judicial powers be consolidated into a burgeoning administrative branch.[13]

Landis's view took hold, and administrative agencies have expanded exponentially ever since.

So, without going through the Article V amendment process, without states getting to vote to ratify or reject this overhaul of the Constitution created by the Founders, the structure of our foundational document was significantly altered to empower unaccountable bureaucrats to run our lives.

The rule of law was abandoned, and the type of "tyranny" feared by the Founders was now expanding across America.

FALLEN ANGELS OF GOVERNMENT

James Madison explained in the *Federalist*, "If men were angels, no government would be necessary. In framing a government which is to be administered by men over men, the great difficulty lies in this: you must first enable the government to control the governed; and in the next place oblige it to control itself."[14]

The Founders intended the rule of law that intertwined the three branches of government to solve that riddle. They constructed a government where people were governed by laws, not by men. And they intertwined the three branches of government to ensure it would "control itself."

Today's Environment

The Founders instilled checks and balances to prevent government from running amok. They created a government that would have to answer to the people. Now much of that original design has been defaced.

With the widespread reach of administrative agencies, you don't know, will never see, and can't influence the people who decide how your life and business are governed. Where's Madison when we need him?

A big part of what I've tried to do during my years as attorney general and governor is to put the administrative genie back in the bottle and return our country to its intended constitutional structure.

For example, I sued the EPA nineteen times because of its egregious actions that far exceed both the Constitution and the authority given it by Congress. It's one of the biggest threats to the rule of law in America.

The Environmental Protection Agency is benignly named. But it has become the very face of tyranny that Madison intended to prevent.

The EPA administrator responsible for the state of Texas actually went so far as to say he wanted to "crucify" some businesses to make examples of them.

You wouldn't believe this unless I put it in quotes. This is what the EPA administrator said on video. This is what happens when unelected bureaucrats hijack our country:

> It was kinda like how the Romans used to conquer those villages in the Mediterranean. They'd go into a little Turkish town somewhere, they'd find the first five guys they saw, and they'd crucify them. And you know, that town was really easy to manage for the next few years.[15]

This is what the fourth branch of government has become: pseudo–Roman conquerors looking for political opposition to crucify. That is what happens when the executive, legislative, and judicial roles are controlled by one unaccountable entity.

Didn't we fight a Revolutionary War to get away from that behavior?

But wait. It gets worse!

In 1970 Congress used the new Clean Air Act to delegate to the EPA the responsibility to establish "standards of performance" for power plants. The law, however, says virtually nothing about what those standards should be. That task was left to the unelected bureaucrats at the EPA.

The 1970 law wasn't designed to curb greenhouse gas emissions. Congress didn't even contemplate the idea at the time it passed the law.

But details like that never stopped an administrative agency from just making up the law. So, more than forty years later, the EPA effectively rewrote the Clean Air Act by applying its own interpretation to impose a massive greenhouse gas regulatory regime.

The EPA interpreted the vague words "standards and performance" in the Clean Air Act to authorize it to impose on America a

1,600-page Clean Power Plan. Notably, that plan has nothing to do with "clean air" or regulating pollutants that could affect your health. Instead, the Clean Power Plan (CPP) targets global warming.

(This book is like the Rosetta Stone of government-speak. Before you finish, you'll learn enough alphabet jargon to visit Washington, D.C., and converse with the locals.)

Even if you accepted—hook, line, and sinker—the EPA's claim that climate change is an urgent threat, the CPP would have virtually no effect on global warming. It would, however, leave an irreparable gash in the collective wallet of America.

Facts quickly surfaced, like they always do.

The EPA had moved far beyond just executing the laws written by Congress. It was now playing the role of energy "central planner" for our country by restructuring how energy is generated and used in America.

And the costs were steep.

Depending on your information source, the CPP price tag is either billions or tens of billions of dollars per year. The CPP would increase the cost of living for all Americans. The cost of goods and services would increase, some businesses would shutter, countless jobs would be lost. America would suffer from higher unemployment, lower economic growth, and pinched incomes. All because of a rogue agency trying to enforce a rule that it created but was never voted on by Congress.

The CPP's reverberations were so loud it achieved something no one thought possible. It galvanized Congress to act. Both the House and the Senate quickly realized the devastation the EPA's CPP (yes, I speak govern-ese, too) would do to the United States.

Remember, the EPA is an agency that gets its authority only to the extent it is delegated by Congress.

The EPA had hijacked Congress's responsibility to make the laws, and Congress didn't like it. The House and Senate quickly passed a joint resolution nullifying the EPA's plan. Specifically, the resolution, dated October 23, 2015, said "such rule shall have no force or effect."

Then, the unthinkable happened.

Ben Franklin, James Madison, Alexander Hamilton—the whole lot of them—would have bet their lives it would never happen. In fact, they pledged their lives to construct a country to prevent it from happening.

With the stroke of a pen, the president vetoed the act of Congress. In doing so he toppled the Constitution itself. By vetoing Congress's nullification of the EPA rule, the president automatically reinstated the administrative agency's rule.

That means that an act of an administrative agency in the "fourth branch" of government, nowhere mentioned in the Constitution, trumped an act of Congress—the Congress that in Article I, Section 1, is given all legislative powers authorized by the Constitution.

REMEMBER HOW THIS CHAPTER BEGAN?

Under the Constitution, which branch of government writes the laws? If you answered "Congress" you got the constitutional question correct. In America today, though, that's not how government works.

With the stroke of a pen, the rule of law was subverted by the rule of man; the principle that the lawmakers must be answerable to the people was deserted. Stacks of regulations were forced on us by unaccountable bureaucrats.

As you might imagine, this didn't sit well in Texas. Or America.

Texas saddled up with twenty-six other states to sue the federal government to end this regulatory stampede. By this time I was governor and so the lawsuit was filed by Texas's new attorney general, Ken Paxton.

Once again, more than half of America was suing America.

Because states and their citizens would have to pay billions of dollars on the front end just to begin the process of trying to comply with the new gargantuan EPA rule, we asked the court for a "stay." This means we asked the court to stop forcing the states to begin complying with the law until we had a chance to fully present our case in court—a process that could take several years.

The court of appeals denied our request.

The new CPP was racing down the regulatory rails until it came to a jolting halt from an unexpected source. On February 9, 2016, the Supreme Court granted our stay.

This means the EPA's massive Power Plan will remain on ice until states and citizens have their day in court.

Regardless of how the final court decision turns out, one thing is clear: the administrative branch of government is breaking America's back.

IT'S COMPLICATED

Yes, law is complicated. But I have a simple solution.

We must return the lawmaking process to Congress as enshrined in Article I.

The way administrative law has evolved, rules like the CPP are commonplace and they have the force of law *unless* they are rejected by Congress.

There are two problems with this. First, it should be your elected representative, accountable to you, who decides which laws govern your lives. Remember the compact between you—the people—and those you give power to govern your lives.

Second, as we saw with the president's veto of Congress's resolution to nullify the CPP, the old concept that agency rules have the force of law unless they are rejected by Congress no longer has vitality. If a president can veto Congress's rejection of an administrative rule, then we've become a nation with a diminished legislative branch and an emboldened administrative branch.

The best solution is to restore first principles of the Constitution. Rules and regulations by administrative agencies like the EPA should have no binding legal force until they are *approved* by Congress.

This forces administrative agencies to work with—and *for*—Congress the way they should.

It also fixes the dubious practice of Congress delegating its lawmaking powers to administrative agencies and empowering unelected bureaucrats to write laws.

The current practice leads to what Nancy Pelosi famously said about Obamacare: "We have to pass the bill so you can find out what is in it." (She said that, by the way, at a speech using a teleprompter.)

Members of Congress truly have no idea what's in the laws they pass because far too much of the law will be added by those unelected bureaucrats. This practice is all too convenient. Congress doesn't have to dirty its hands with all the pesky details, while at the same time it is able to deflect criticism about regulations. "It's those darn regulators," they often say, without taking action to restrain those agencies.

Rather than trying to keep up with complex legal gymnastics, let's do what the Founders did. It's called the KISS rule. You know it. The Founders didn't know it by that name, but they achieved it.

Keep it simple, stupid. And keep the intended constitutional structure that forces the person you elect to be accountable for the laws you have to live by.

IT DOESN'T HAVE TO BE COMPLICATED

Some people may wonder about amending the Constitution.

On the other hand, I don't see how you can read this chapter without realizing that the Constitution has, for all practical purposes, been amended to add the administrative branch of government, without you having a say in the process, and probably without you even knowing it.

And with every passing month, these "amendments" become solidified into laws—laws that affect you and me.

Some people who've already bought into the current system, or been bought *by* it, might argue that our modern administrative process is the natural by-product of a complex society that the Founders couldn't have foreseen.

To the contrary, the Founders did understand that a growing America would need a Constitution that could grow with it. That's exactly why they inserted Article V into the Constitution, so we can amend it as needed. But amend it democratically; not autocratically or bureaucratically.

Others will contend that we can't return to a strict application of the nondelegation doctrine that was intended by the Founders. They think it would be unworkable if Congress and the courts had to do all the decision making without being able to delegate the task to administrative agencies.

The fact is, courts grapple with difficult issues all the time involving complex constitutional issues like what constitutes due process of law, or equal protection of the laws, or a reasonable search and seizure.

These issues protected by the Bill of Rights have evolved in ways the Founders couldn't have foreseen. Did the Founders foresee how to apply search and seizure laws to an iPhone? Of course not. Do we need administrative agencies to write rules to govern such issues? Absolutely not!

Just as the Bill of Rights is a part of the Constitution, so is Article I, Section 1. It should be the elected and accountable members of Congress who decide the laws that govern our lives.

In the twenty-first century, is it still possible to have a nondelegation doctrine? You bet.

States like Texas—which is far more populous and more commercially complex than all the original thirteen states combined—still have it.

By one count, there are eighteen other states that still apply the nondelegation doctrine: Arizona, Florida, Illinois, Kentucky, Massachusetts, Montana, Nebraska, Nevada, New Hampshire, New Mexico, New York, Ohio, Oklahoma, Pennsylvania, South Carolina, South Dakota, Virginia, and West Virginia.[16]

The legislative process established by the Founders, and written in the Constitution, still works. My proposal restores that plan by requiring elected lawmakers, not unaccountable bureaucrats, to make the laws you live under.

Busier Congress and Quieter President

We've watched a president create "laws" with a pen and a phone. Perhaps more disturbing is what we haven't witnessed behind the scenes—the thousands upon thousands of laws, rules, and regulations cranked out by unknown bureaucrats telling you what to do.

My proposal ends that. No administrative regulation would have effect unless approved by Congress. The administrative branch can administer without Congress, meaning they can perform their constitutionally oriented function of helping the president execute the laws. But they can't make those laws. That's Congress's job.

Remember President Obama excusing his executive actions because "where Congress won't act, I will"? [17] And in acting, he assumed authority he did not have under the Constitution by altering immigration laws.

My proposal forces the issue right back into the constitutional paradigm—back in the hands of Congress.

There are at least 535 people in America who might not like this change very much: members of Congress. They would suddenly get a lot busier, having actual laws to vote on. They're going to have to read bills and regulations. They're going to have to make decisions. They will be more directly accountable for the decisions issued from Washington, D.C.

Sounds refreshing—and constitutional.

Eleven

Commerce Claws

Property must be secured or Liberty cannot exist.
—JOHN ADAMS

Elected officials are up for unemployment every few years. You probably noticed.

If you want to serve the public you have to give them a reason to hire you. I figured that if you're going to run for office, it should be for a cause—not just because.

Every campaign I ran, and every day I served in office, has been focused on priorities.

When I ran for state district judge in Harris County and when I twice ran for the Texas Supreme Court position to which Governor Bush initially appointed me, the priority was to apply the law as written, give everyone a fair hearing, and rule promptly with solid reasoning behind the decision.

When I ran for attorney general my priority was to use the law to make Texas a better and safer place, while also fighting a federal government that was increasingly intent on circumventing the law.

I ran for governor to keep Texas the best state in America. (My apologies to readers from the other forty-nine states. But y'all are welcome here any time.) I'm fond of saying, "There are two kinds of people in this world: Texans, and those who wish they were Texans."

State pride is a good thing. In fact, it drives my priorities as governor. Keep Texas safe by supporting law enforcement and securing the border. Keep Texas prosperous and grow jobs by cutting taxes and reducing regulations. Improve our schools from early education through higher education. Make our infrastructure the best in America by investing in roads without raising taxes, fees, tolls, or debt.

My campaign for governor produced an effective television commercial to show my priority to build roads. I was filmed next to congested rush hour traffic in Dallas. While pushing my wheelchair past a line of bumper-to-bumper cars, I looked into the camera and explained: "A guy in a wheelchair can go faster than traffic on our clogged roads. Elect me governor and I'll get Texas moving again."

It worked for the campaign and for the following legislative session, which appropriated the money needed to make Texas roads the best.

But anyone who's worked for me knows that I have another set of priorities that rank even higher: my commitment to God and to my family.

My wife and I enjoy going to the same church we started attending when we were dating in the late 1970s.

When it comes to our daughter, Audrey, I followed the advice I got when she was an infant: "Spend every minute you can with your child because before you know it, she will be gone."

In typical style, I immersed myself in books about the subject of parenthood. I still have the dozens of books I read about raising children and helping them through their school years. By the way, my favorite, which I read, reread, and have repeatedly recommended to others, is *Strong Fathers, Strong Daughters: 10 Secrets Every Father Should Know*, by Meg Meeker.

More important, I put into practice what I read.

My staff knew that Audrey was a priority. Until my campaign for governor—when Audrey was a high school junior—we had an inflexible rule: I would never be away from home more than two evenings a week.

The speaking requests were endless, the to-do list daunting, requests for my time ceaseless; but we had our priorities.

I made sure I was home to read Audrey bedtime stories. We were regulars at Chuck E. Cheese's pizza. During her elementary school years, we had daddy-daughter dates on Fridays, going to a movie and then next door to Amy's Ice Cream.

I never missed a birthday, recital, or meaningful milestone event. In fact, I was often the carpool driver for those events.

On my desk in the Capitol is the picture of when we first went fishing. On the wall at my campaign office is the trophy from our first hunting trip. Different people have different skills. Audrey is a natural at using a rifle or a shotgun.

I loved every minute of it. Audrey did, too, except for one thing she totally disdained. Whenever she had school tests, I prepared written questions to prep her. She hated having to go through those drills, from elementary school to high school. But I insisted. There are priorities.

I've juggled many priorities in life that flowed from a lot of different titles—Judge, Justice, Attorney General, and Governor. But the title I cherish most, is Dad.

By sticking to priorities, the whole family graduated the same year. The year Audrey graduated from high school and went on to college is the same year that Cecilia and I graduated from the attorney general's office to the governor's office.

RACING TO THE FINISH

Many people are familiar with big, formal, presidential campaign events—large venues, fancy platforms, big guys in sunglasses talking into their sleeves, and lots of staff running around trying to control the chaos.

In my first run for attorney general in 2002, I had a one-person entourage. At various times, Daniel Hodge was my travel aide, security detail, advance staff, wheelchair fixer, press secretary, bumpersticker wrangler, and a multitude of other titles.

As the campaign was nearing the end we stopped in Amarillo for an event. A friend of Daniel's was driving us around in his mother's car. Glamorous. We parked at the event, where our driver went to the trunk to retrieve my wheelchair.

"Uh-oh," came his voice from the back of the car. The button for the trunk had broken off. He started banging and tugging on the lid, then scrambled for something to pry the trunk open. Meanwhile, the media was beginning to close in on us.

Finally, Daniel suggested we use the key to open the trunk. This man is still one of my top aides. Hard work and common sense will get you a long way in life.

In Texas we have an early voting period that ends a few days before the election. By that time, I was told I had a comfortable lead in the polls. But I take nothing for granted. It had been drilled into me since my youth that you *never* stop running until you cross the goal line.

So we kept our schedule, barnstorming the state to urge every last voter to side with me.

Our last stop was Abilene. I believe in asking people for their vote. So I sat in my wheelchair outside a local polling place to shake voters' hands and urge them to vote for me, until daylight turned to darkness on a cold November evening.

And it was raining.

That's been our style in every campaign—sprint to the finish.

Cecilia's Campaign

My wife also made our family a priority as her career advanced.

Cecilia is the granddaughter of immigrants from Monterrey, Mexico. Both of Cecilia's parents were educators, and they instilled in Cecilia, her sister, and her two brothers a love of learning and helping others.

She loved learning so much she earned three college degrees: a bachelor's degree in psychology, a master's degree in education, and a master's degree in theology, all from the University of St. Thomas, in Houston.

Cecilia followed her passion and became a teacher, vice principal, and principal at several Catholic schools across Texas. She later went on to another noble calling, working to help seniors as the managing director of community relations for an adult health care service provider.

Part of her job there, which she loved, was managing a benevolent fund to aid employees who desperately needed help.

For example, families with a sick child in the hospital sometimes needed a place to stay while their child was receiving medical treatment. The fund paid the rent. In other emergencies, families received help with funeral expenses, or cleanup after floods or tornadoes. It was almost like the role of a Red Cross worker, helping others in their time of need.

"This is hard work, but it feels like we're doing God's work, you know?" she would tell Audrey and me at the dinner table.

With some sadness, she left that job to join me on the gubernatorial campaign trail. She soon saw, however, the vision not only of ensuring Texas remained the lodestar for America, but of how she could expand the way she helps others in a new role: the first lady of Texas.

She has exceeded even her own expectations. She's hugged Texans who just lost their home to a tornado, she's aided victims of a horrific flood, she's read books to students in elementary school. And she's repeatedly done something she swore she would never do: she's given speeches.

You'll never meet a more genuine, bighearted, caring person than Cecilia. I often hear about someone who's approached her during an event or after a speech: "You're so real," they say. She shrugs and wonders, *What were you expecting?* She truly loves to engage with people, hear their stories, see their photos, and especially pet their dogs.

As first lady, Cecilia no longer drives. Instead, our security detail drives her everywhere she goes. But that hasn't stopped Cecilia from a Friday ritual that began long before the campaign for governor. For years she has been delivering hot meals to the elderly, disabled, and homebound with the organization Meals on Wheels. She continues that labor of love in her new role as first lady of Texas.

"I may be the only person they talk with that day," she says. "It's so much more than just delivering meals."

Cecilia knows her priorities. For her, they come from the heart.

Once a Judge . . .

I often begin speeches with a story, to lighten up the crowd, but also to let them know something more substantial is coming.

During my tenure as a justice on the Texas Supreme Court, I sometimes spoke at large conferences for attorneys.

On one of those occasions, I entered the back of the room just before I was scheduled to speak.

I wanted to get a feel for the audience, so I rolled up next to a stranger and asked him how the conference was going.

"Well, it's going okay, but you know how these things go. The next speaker is another one of those long-winded judges."

I asked him, "Do you know who I am?"

"I have no idea," he said matter-of-factly.

"I'm Judge Greg Abbott, and I'm the next speaker."

You could tell he was embarrassed. But, being a quick-thinking lawyer, he responded, "Well, do you know who I am?"

"I have no idea," I replied.

"Great, I'm outta here!" And he was.

With that story, here's my encouragement. As a long-winded judge, I'm about to take you through an incredibly important constitutional issue. See for yourself how the Constitution was dismantled, and the impact this trend has on your life, your property, and your family.

Homework

I always enjoyed helping our daughter Audrey with her homework. Still do.

Whether they admit it or not, children want—and need—help with their schoolwork. One of the reasons kids need guidance is that they can be easily distracted by anything *but* homework. Part of our job as parents is to help children focus.

Congress has a problem with focus, too.

It seems they want to get involved in everything except their sworn duties. These lawmakers cannot be relied upon to do something as mundane as pass an annual budget, much less balance one. And as if the problems facing our country weren't interesting enough, Congress often wants to dig its claws into every state's business.

As Texas attorney general, and now as governor, I've seen Congress continue to regulate activities that are limited within a state's borders—*intra*state activity and commerce. That violates the limits on Congress's authority.

The executive branch is rightly criticized for expanding administrative agencies far beyond what the Constitution provides. But Congress is a willing accomplice in this constitutional commandeering. Like the "aider and abettor" who gives matches and gasoline to an arsonist, Congress joined forces with the executive branch to torch the Constitution.

Congress clearly shirked its constitutional duty to make the laws by delegating this ability to unelected bureaucrats at federal agencies like the EPA. It's like a student who refuses to do his homework and demands his neighbor do it for him.

One reason why Congress's approval ratings has plummeted to 11 percent[1] (a whopping 86 percent of the public say they disapprove of its performance) is that they aren't doing the job the Constitution requires them to do—the job you elected them to do.

They've failed to pass a budget, failed to pass a border security plan, failed to block an overreaching executive branch, and failed to overturn or correct misguided Supreme Court decisions.

Despite the public's frustration with Congress not doing its job, Americans often grow even angrier when Congress actually *passes* a law. Often an act of Congress is a harbinger of carnage for your freedom and your wallet.

The weapon of choice used by Congress to inflict the most damage to American families and businesses, and the greatest devastation to our constitutional design, is the Commerce Clause.

But that's not what the Founders intended.

LIMITS BRING FREEDOM

Unlike many other countries, the guiding document in the United States limits the federal government's authority to run your life. This enshrines into our foundation the principle that makes America different from—and superior to—other countries.

The real power rests with the people—not with government control. That principle is what allows you the freedom to achieve success, limited only by the size of your dreams, not by the size of your government.

The Constitution was written to *limit* Congress's ability to run your life.

That's what the Constitution means when it says: "All legislative Powers *herein granted* shall be vested in a Congress."

The highlighted words show that the people of the United States gave to Congress *only* the powers that are specifically referenced in the Constitution, and nothing more. In other words, Congress can pass laws only to the extent it has been authorized to do so by the Constitution itself.

Remember former House Speaker Nancy Pelosi's indignant response when she was questioned about which constitutional provision authorized Congress to force Americans to buy health care insurance under Obamacare?

Her response explains a lot about contemporary Congress. She derisively replied: "Are you serious?"

The twenty-first-century Congress considers its power to impose laws on you to be unlimited.

Nowhere has that power grab been more extreme or coercive than Congress's abuse of the Commerce Clause.

There's a reason for that. Over the past century, Congress—with a substantial assist by the courts—has been enabled to expand the scope of the Commerce Clause to pass laws far beyond what the Founders intended.

The Commerce Clause is simple. It gives Congress the power to "regulate Commerce with foreign Nations, and among the several States, and with the Indian tribes."

You can plainly see that Congress wasn't granted the authority to regulate all commerce, let alone all activity. The power given to Congress to regulate commerce was limited only to commerce with foreign nations, Indian tribes, and interstate commercial activity.

Clearly the Commerce Clause did not give Congress the authority to regulate "*intra*state" commerce or activity. (Intrastate commerce is commercial activity that occurs entirely within the confines of one state alone.) Nevertheless, Congress has taken the straightforward words of the Commerce Clause and used it to expand its power to regulate every conceivable activity—and even inactivity—regardless of whether it dealt with commerce of any kind, and regardless of whether the activity is interstate, international, or occurs only in one state.

COURTING DISASTER

The authors of the Commerce Clause considered "commerce" to mean "trade" or "exchange of goods." And that's probably how you would define the term today.[2]

For most of our nation's history, that's the way the Commerce Clause was applied—as pertaining to trade between states and with foreign nations and Native American tribes.

In 1824, the Supreme Court applied the plain wording of the Constitution to rule that the Commerce Clause did not give Congress broad regulatory power, nor did it give Congress the power to regulate "intrastate" commerce.[3]

This straightforward application of the Commerce Clause largely continued through the remainder of the 1800s.

Then, in the 1930s, the Constitution was effectively rewritten in a matter of a few years. What happened then is the crux of every challenge discussed in this book.

For half of our nation's history, the Constitution was predominately applied based on its clear wording and the courts followed the intent of its authors. But in the 1930s broad swaths of the Constitution were redesigned by Washington insiders.

If the Constitution is to be changed, there is a process for that. It's contained in Article V, which describes how to amend it. Importantly, the Constitution was intended to be amended only after giving the people of the United States a say in the process. That is the ratification process. Unless three-fourths of the states agree, the Constitution cannot be amended.

That process was ignored by the Supreme Court when, on its own, it altered how the Constitution was to be applied. Look at what happened in a matter of just two years.

In 1935, the Court ruled that Congress was wrong to regulate the hours and wages of employees of an *intrastate* business because the activity being regulated did not involve interstate commerce. The Court ruled that Congress had the power to regulate activities that affected interstate commerce but did not have the power to regulate intrastate commerce.

In their decision, the Court forebodingly explained that without this distinction between intrastate and interstate commerce "there would be *virtually no limit to the federal power* and for all practical purposes we should have a completely centralized government." The Court's concern soon became reality.[4]

Then came the heavy hand of FDR and his threat to "pack" the Court.

The Constitution hadn't changed. But Supreme Court justices had changed their minds.

Just two years after denying Congress the ability to regulate *intrastate* commerce, the Supreme Court suddenly began allowing it. And once the dam was broken, the legal landscape was flooded with wave upon wave of new laws, rules, and regulations.[5]

Rather than construing "commerce" in the Constitution to be associated with interstate trade, as intended, the Court began allowing Congress to regulate virtually any and all activities, regardless of whether they involved trade, and regardless of whether the activity crossed state lines.

The politics of the Great Depression, the New Deal, and FDR

himself convinced Congress and the Supreme Court to alter the historical application of the Commerce Clause. Suddenly there was mounting pressure for Congress to fabricate schemes to create a more centralized federal government.

And the Supreme Court aided Congress by abandoning its own past decisions about the Commerce Clause and ignoring the clear limits on that constitutional power. The Court began a new era of allowing Congress to pass virtually any law it desired, using the Commerce Clause as its basis.

But it gets worse.

In 1941, the Supreme Court directly reworded the Constitution. In *United States v. Darby*, it wrote: "The power of Congress over interstate commerce is not confined to the regulation of commerce among the states." [6]

Compare that sentence to what the Constitution actually says where it empowers Congress "to regulate commerce among the several states." Remember both Madison and the Constitution commanded: powers not granted in the Constitution are denied. Remember that the Tenth Amendment teaches that "powers not delegated to the United States by the Constitution" are reserved to the states or to the people. Contrary to what the Supreme Court wrote in *Darby*, the power the Constitution gave to Congress over interstate commerce was specifically confined to the regulation of commerce among the states.

The following year, in *Wickard v. Filburn*, the Supreme Court issued one of its most egregious decisions that thrust broad power into Congress's hands and destroyed private property rights and American freedom. [7]

In that one decision, the Supreme Court displayed both the evils of a centralized government and the consequences of a Congress unrestrained by constitutional limits.

SOWING AND REAPING

Roscoe Filburn was an Ohio farmer who grew wheat to feed animals on his own farm. He didn't sell his wheat to others and his crop didn't cross state lines. Filburn's wheat was never commerce, much less interstate commerce.

But that didn't stop Congress. It wanted to regulate how much wheat farmers could grow so it could control the price of wheat. Is that what America had become? The land of the free had transformed into the home of government control of markets.

The Supreme Court upheld Congress's Agriculture Adjustment Act, which empowered the federal government to limit how much wheat farmers could grow. In doing so, the Court put a dagger through the limits embedded in the Commerce Clause.

The Supreme Court ruled that even though Filburn's wheat farming is "local" and even though "it may not be regarded as commerce, it may still, whatever its nature, be reached by Congress."

That ruling gave Congress the license it needed to regulate anything, *"whatever its nature."*

After *Wickard v. Filburn,* the die was cast, and both Congress and the courts viewed the Commerce Clause as an empowering clause to limitless regulation, rather than a limitation on regulation as written by the Constitution's authors.

Congress began viewing the Commerce Clause as unhinged from commercial activity and began using it to regulate actions that had nothing to do with commerce or interstate activity. Congress even considered the clause as authority to regulate freedom itself—like an American's decision not to buy health insurance.

In the Obamacare law, Congress wasn't regulating commercial activity. Instead it was forcing Americans into the stream of commerce by compelling them to buy a product against their will and then regulating them.

The Founders would be shocked by America's new "central planning." Karl Marx would be impressed.

With every heavy-handed regulation, Congress created a new government paradigm that put lids on the aspiration of Americans to dream big, and work hard to achieve those dreams.

Congress used the Commerce Clause as its power to impose Obamacare and it crushed the aspiration of doctors who preferred to treat patients rather than fill out paperwork. Similarly, Congress's use of the Commerce Clause to impose harsh regulations under laws like Dodd-Frank, and through agencies like the EPA, has stymied aspirations of lenders to stimulate the economy, of manufacturers to build more products, and of entrepreneurs seeking to start and grow a business.

ENDANGERED DREAMERS

When I was in law school, there was a poster on the front door where my wife worked. It read:

Without dreams, there is no need to work.
Without work, there is no need to dream.

I reflected on these words from time to time as motivation to dream big and work hard. But government has changed so much since those days that it's now threatening to eclipse that type of motivation. We can't let that happen.

There was a reason why Congress thought it could get away with this scandalous revision of constitutional principles. A reason why Nancy Pelosi was shocked that someone would have the gall to question her about which part of the Constitution Obamacare was based on. Courts had not been doing their job to limit Congress's power the way the Founders intended.

For example, courts had allowed Congress to misapply the Commerce Clause to regulate your lives and hijack your freedom through the Endangered Species Act. It was passed in 1973 and was the culmination of Congress's newfound belief that it could regulate whatever it wanted.

Once regulators declare a species endangered, you can hope for only one thing: the species is not on your property. If it is, you will forever be a subject and the species will be your master. Your private property—the property that John Adams said "must be secured or Liberty cannot exist"—will be controlled by a spider, or even a fly.

If you are like most Americans, there are flies on your property. It happens. This isn't surprising because there are more than one hundred thousand species of flies, according to some estimates.[8] There are so many fly species that every man, woman, and child in Green Bay, Wisconsin, could name their own species, with some left over.

Can the federal government regulate your property if there are flies on it? By now you know the answer.

The day before groundbreaking was scheduled for a new "state-of-the-art," "earthquake-proof" hospital in San Bernardino County, California, the U.S. Fish and Wildlife Service added another fly to the endangered species list. The fly lives for only two weeks before dying and exists only in the forty-square-mile area where the hospital was planned. Building the hospital as intended would violate federal law because it threatened "six to eight flies."[9]

The county and other parties sued, claiming that the Commerce Clause can't possibly empower Congress to regulate flies that never cross state lines and are not sold commercially. They lost at every court along the way, and the U.S. Supreme Court allowed the Court of Appeals decision to stand.

As Judge David Sentelle of the U.S. Court of Appeals in Washington, D.C., explained in a dissenting opinion, "At one point, the [U.S. Fish and Wildlife] Service threatened to require shutting down the eight-lane San Bernardino Freeway (U.S. 10, one of the most heavily traveled in southern California) for two months every year (I am not making this up)." [10]

Judge Sentelle captured the new frontier of constitutional overreach: "So wide-ranging has been the application of the Clause as to prompt one writer to 'wonder why anyone would make the mistake of calling it the Commerce Clause instead of the 'hey-you-can-do-whatever-you-feel-like clause.' " [11]

In Texas, we have our own tiny problems, too.

ALONG CAME A SPIDER

San Antonio is one of the many fast-growing cities in Texas. Jobs are plentiful, families are becoming more prosperous, and traffic congestion is growing with the population. Finally, the Texas Department of Transportation was building an underpass that would relieve congestion at a San Antonio intersection clogged with about eighty thousand vehicles a day. That is, until a spider on the endangered species list was found during construction. (If nothing else, you have to be impressed with their attention to detail.)

Before this discovery, the spider in question was last seen miles away about thirty years earlier. The spider has no commercial use and doesn't crawl across state lines. That doesn't, however, stop the federal government from stepping in.

Now that the spider resurfaced, it was blocking the future of Texans. But the federal government found a quick and easy solution: spend more taxpayer dollars. That's always the solution from Washington, D.C. Rather than build the planned underpass, the federal government "allowed" Texas to build an overpass that cost about three times as much as originally planned.[12]

In another example, fellow Texan John Yearwood has run a small business on his property for decades. Recently, he offered to let a local 4-H club use some of his land for camping and other related activities.

Sounds fine, right? Well, the property is also home to a little-known spider, the "Bone Cave Harvestman," which is known to live only in Texas. It's also considered endangered, under the Endangered Species Act.

Because these spiders might be harmed by the little campers, federal authorities prohibited Yearwood from allowing 4-H kids to use his property. Not only that, but he is now threatened with enormous fines for disturbing the spiders.[13]

Maybe we need to add "property owners" to the endangered species list.

The Endangered Species Act exists only because Congress abused its authority under the Commerce Clause. The only things that should be endangered are the careers of representatives who vote for laws like the Endangered Species Act.

Many people in America dream about the opportunity to own private property. This aspiration is being crushed—along with a fundamental premise of the American Dream—by the federal government's unapologetic expansion of the Commerce Clause to take and control private property.

Congress needs to focus on its role in government and do its own homework.

Removing the Claws

I'm as baffled as Madison and the Framers would be that anyone in the federal government could use the Commerce Clause to meddle in intrastate business and private property.

But as the saying goes, *What a tangled web we weave* . . .

To fix Congress's overreaching ways, I propose amending the Commerce Clause to restore its original intent and deny Congress the authority to regulate activities that occur only in one state.

The modified language of Article I, Section 8 would look like this:

> To regulate Commerce with foreign Nations, and among the several States, and with the Indian tribes, *and prohibit Congress from regulating any activity, which occurs wholly within one State.*

The wording allows Congress to continue regulating activities among the states that clearly involve interstate commerce, such as interstate highways and traffic, borders, airwaves, and things that pass over and through them.

But Congress would no longer be able to regulate activities like a farmer who just wants to grow and eat his own food. And Congress could never again threaten to force you to buy something you don't want.

HOMEWORK AND PRIORITIES

Several justices and members of Congress are published authors, and I congratulate them. But they should focus their writing on books and legal opinions—and stay away from editing the Constitution. Maybe try poetry.

Here's my attempt at poetic injustice:

Little Miss Muffet
Sat on a tuffet (On her property),
Eating her curds and whey (Just eating, not selling),
Along came a spider,
Federal agents beside her,
And frightened Miss Muffet away.

Let's be clear, some federal regulation is authorized by the Constitution. But Congress has far exceeded that authority.

The clear wording, and purpose, of the Commerce Clause gives Congress the power to regulate interstate commerce—trade between states. Amending the Constitution to "prohibit Congress from regulating any activity, which occurs wholly within one state" will restore to the states the power to regulate intrastate commerce.

Imagine a country where all laws are created by Congress as opposed to bureaucratic agencies, and the Commerce Clause is applied as intended.

Imagine a Congress focused on its homework.

Twelve

Of Groceries and Governments

. . . to preserve our independence, we must not
let our rulers load us with perpetual debt.
—THOMAS JEFFERSON

When I have the opportunity to speak with a new group of people, I sometimes tell the story of my 1984 accident. Even today, some are surprised to see me in a wheelchair, and many haven't heard about how the injury happened.

As I relate the details of the split second that changed my life, people imagine the scene and shake their heads. I can almost hear them wondering, *How SLOW was this guy jogging to get hit by a tree?!*

I'm no stranger to doubtful questions, especially in my campaigns for public service. Some people doubted my ability to run—for office, that is. But no one ever questioned my resolve.

And I suppose the serious answer to the funny question is: I was focused on what was ahead of me.

SKATING FORWARD

Sorry, Dallas Stars fans, I prefer football to hockey. But I am a fan of NHL legend Wayne Gretzky and his advice about hockey and life.

"A good hockey player plays where the puck is. A great hockey player plays where the puck is going to be."

That's a pretty good way of describing how I tried to focus my career.

Years earlier, during physical rehabilitation, I made the decision not to focus my energies on walking but instead, to go directly to work. Instead of getting bogged down in wrestling with what had happened to me, I was resolved to make the best of my life in my new condition. Ever since that day I had a clear vision to move forward.

There are no rearview mirrors on my wheelchair.

As a Texas Supreme Court judge, my decision to run for attorney general was based on a desire to aggressively pursue important issues, not wait for them to arrive in my courtroom. The same was true in my run for governor. As the longest-serving attorney general in Texas history, I was ready to take on new challenges in an executive role to focus on policies that will keep Texas a bastion of freedom.

During my campaign, Texans would tell me every day they were glad I was running for governor, but they sure would miss me filing all those lawsuits against President Obama. I reassured them, "Don't worry, I'm just moving from a general in the battlefield to be commander in chief. I'll keep fighting for freedom against the federal government."

Instead of looking through the rearview mirror, and making decisions based on the past, I decided to help the people of Texas enjoy better lives by insisting on the rule of law.

UNEXPECTED

I entered the political fray to fix things and help people.

Ever since my days in private law practice, protecting children has always been especially important to me.

Cecilia and I always dreamed of having a child. Unfortunately, it didn't happen.

On the positive side, we have the privilege of being godparents to almost twenty children. Yes, we were a popular choice for that honor back in the day.

Now we can't imagine our lives without our daughter. The child we never expected.

In 1996, I was in my first election campaign for the Texas Supreme Court, the position to which Governor Bush appointed me. The appointment meant we had to move to Austin. Cecilia left her job as a principal in Houston and, fortunately, found another principal position in our new hometown.

After moving to Austin, we began talking about the possibility of adopting a baby. Cecilia explored all the options while I deep-dived into learning all about it.

The possibility caused both excitement and anxiety. We visited and applied to several adoption homes. And we waited.

One day we received an unexpected phone call, and an unexpected question. A friend of a friend's daughter was pregnant and was considering giving the child up for adoption.

"Would you and Cecilia like to meet the mother and father?" our friend asked.

"Um. Yes," was our stunned reply.

A few days later we met with the young couple. This was a difficult decision for them and the only comfort they could gain would be knowing their child would be in a loving home.

The meeting went well—or so we thought. We certainly didn't have any prior experience meeting birth parents. But when they told us they were also interviewing other prospective parents, our hearts sank.

Several weeks passed, and we heard nothing from the couple. We tried, unsuccessfully, to forget the whole matter and continue exploring other options—until we received another phone call from the friend of a friend who made the initial call. We were invited back to another meeting in October 1996.

The meeting turned out to be a baby shower—for us!—given by the expecting parents and their friends who introduced us. It was there we received the news they'd chosen us to raise the child. You can imagine our surprise, but can't imagine our happiness.

They gave Cecilia an "I'm expecting" button to wear, and she beamed with a smile I hadn't seen for a while. I suppose the same was true for my smile.

From that day we began the journey of parenthood, going to doctor appointments with the birth mother, meetings with social workers, hearings with adoption judges, and preparing for a new season of life.

February 13 at four o'clock in the morning, we got the call. Our daughter was born that afternoon, and I was the first person to hold her. We named her Audrey, after Cecilia's sixth-grade teacher.

WHEELING AUDREY

The next day, on Valentine's Day, we brought Audrey home. She was wearing a white onesie with red hearts all over it.

We were sure we had the most beautiful baby in the world. And the people in the hospital, staff and visitors alike, seemed to agree. Strongly.

In fact, the smiles and stares we received seemed a bit much, until we looked at the photos from that day. There I was in my wheelchair, holding our new baby, being pushed by a nurse, while Cecilia walked along beside us.

Not the usual parental procession leaving a hospital.

On that day, I became a better husband and a better man. I also became a better public servant. From the moment Cecilia and I first held Audrey, we saw our work through the lens of "How can we make the world a better place for her and her generation?"

DRIVEN

For Cecilia and me, one of the biggest changes since becoming governor has been the fact that neither of us is allowed to drive.

I probably shouldn't say this, but before 2015, we'd often drive to the same destination—separately. Let's just say we both have a love for driving and our own particular driving style. Or maybe it's my independent spirit. Which is why my staff refers to me as "communication director" and "chief speechwriter," and is constantly panicked about my personal Twitter account.

If you want to see a governor who writes his own tweets, go to GregAbbott.com for my personal account. (Caution: there's another Greg Abbott on Twitter who is a soccer coach halfway across the globe. I'm often awakened by angry tweets from irate soccer fans—and liberal insomniacs.)

As attorney general, I resisted letting security drive me around.

And I drove *them* crazy. They'd never know when the garage door would suddenly open and my car would come zipping out like the Batmobile from the Batcave.

"You know what?" I told them. "I want to drive to work and go to the grocery store like everybody does."

Believe it or not, until becoming governor, I was the chief grocery shopper in our family. I actually enjoyed it. Audrey and I went to Randall's grocery store almost every week. In fact, if I ever showed up without my daughter, all I heard during my visit was "Where's little Audrey today?"

During debate preparation for governor, I never had to be coached about how much a gallon of milk cost. I shopped every week, checking prices and expiration dates. I understand budgets, and the importance of spending less than you make.

I've also learned about the high cost of higher education. Audrey is now in college, and tuition is taking its toll. In addition, there are shoes for this, a dress for that, a special event here, a needed purchase there. After a while, I had to say "Whoa!" We have to live within a budget.

I told her about an old Texas saying: *If your outflow exceeds your income, your upkeep will be your downfall.*

Spending Clause

Congress needs to learn that lesson. Their endless spending has saddled us with $19 trillion in debt with no end in sight.

To put that debt in context, if the federal government paid it down at the rate of a billion dollars a day, it would take more than fifty years to pay it off.

Another way to look at it: if every individual and business in the United States sent every single penny they earned last year to the U.S. Treasury, we still couldn't repay the federal debt.

This debt is a lid on the future of America. Our record debt is one of the greatest threats to our freedom. It leads to higher taxes, weaker national security, crumbling infrastructure, and less capital available to expand businesses that create jobs.

Thomas Jefferson was right when he warned our young nation: "to preserve our independence, we must not let our rulers load us with perpetual debt." [1]

Congress acts like milk comes from a grocery store. They use the same illusion to make you think Medicaid and Medicare come from pixie dust.

Just like milk really comes from cows, all federal spending programs are milked from taxpayers. Every federal spending program creeps closer to a dangerous cliff with each additional dollar we sink into debt.

Families balance their budgets to remain financially secure. So do states. The federal government must do it, too.

We should consider Thomas Jefferson's guidance from 1798: "I wish it were possible to obtain a single amendment to the Constitution . . . an additional article taking from the federal government the power of borrowing." [2]

Rather than prohibiting debt altogether, I suggest we amend the Constitution to require Congress to balance its budget. They need to know the difference between the Spending Clause and Santa Claus. And Congress needs to know that a balanced budget is on our wish list.

How did we dig this hole? By abandoning the Constitution.

Congress uses the Spending Clause of the Constitution to spend your money. That clause gives Congress the power to "lay and collect Taxes, Duties, Imposts and Excises, to pay the Debts and provide for the common Defence and general Welfare of the United States." (For inquiring minds, the Spending Clause is the first clause of Article I, Section 8 in the Constitution.)

This clause was inserted to *limit* spending. Instead, Congress has used the Spending Clause like a stolen credit card, doing whatever it wants with federal tax dollars. By the way, they stole the credit card from you—and you're on the hook for the balance!

When spending was discussed at the Constitutional Convention and during the ratification process, the Framers emphasized that the purpose of the clause was to place limits on Congress's spending.

Madison wrote that, far from giving Congress "an unlimited commission to exercise every power which may be alleged to be necessary for the common defense or general welfare," the Spending Clause allowed Congress to spend money *only* on what was listed in the Constitution. He emphasized that to think otherwise would be a "misconstruction."[3]

Congress is obviously misconstruing its constitutional authority because it is spending your money on whatever it wants.

GRACE PERIOD

The very first Congress was the first to apply the Spending Clause. That Congress was close in time to the Constitution's ratification and obviously had a firm grasp of what the document intended.

In 1790, the American Glass Manufacturing Company wanted a loan from Congress, much like in 2008, when banks asked Congress to bail them out of debt.

The first Congress, which included members who wrote the Constitution, denied the loan request because the Constitution didn't give them the power to spend money on such bailouts.[4]

Congress continued to correctly apply the Spending Clause limits even in the face of more pressing challenges. In 1796, Savannah, Georgia, was destroyed by a fire. A congressman at the time considered it the most "calamitous" event in the history of the United States.

Despite the devastation, Congress again rejected a request for a bailout because it wasn't authorized by the Spending Clause.

Representative Nathaniel Bacon explained Congress's reasoning. "The sufferings of the people of Savannah were doubtless very great; no one could help feeling for them. But he wished gentlemen to put their finger upon that part of the Constitution which gave that House power to afford them relief."[5]

Without constitutional authority, Congress wouldn't act. Americans had just fought a war to free themselves from a government that imposed the rule of man over the rule of law. They knew better than to allow personal feelings, no matter how well intentioned, to trump the stability that comes with the rule of law.

New Deal

The Spending Clause's limited scope was largely upheld until the time of FDR, when it came to an abrupt end. Just as with the federal government's expansion of the Commerce Clause and the expansion of the administrative branch of government, the Spending Clause was effectively rewritten while FDR was president.

In the 1930s, the United States had to respond to the Great Depression. The deeper question was whether our nation's leaders were going to adopt constitutional solutions, or just disregard the document.

I've mentioned before the lesson I learned when confronting a substantial challenge. I realized that our lives are not defined by how we're challenged, but how we respond to those challenges.

By abandoning the Constitution in a challenging time, our leaders altered the arc of American history by putting the country on a course that empowered government to dispense with the rule of law, and to run your life the way it does today.

Like the fourth Congress, which considered whether to bail out Savannah, all three branches of government had to consider whether to bail out the American economy from the Great Depression. But unlike the early Congress. which carefully heeded its limitations, Congress in the 1930s boldly bounded over those limitations.

Their solutions may have abated the symptoms of the Depression for a while, but it came at the steep price of sacrificing the core principle of our country: freedom.

The great irony is that the stock market had already bottomed out *before* FDR was elected and had risen 200–300 percent *before* many of his programs were implemented.[6] But the big-government genie was out of the bottle.

As mentioned in the previous chapter, 1937 is the year the Supreme Court changed its position about the Commerce Clause and allowed Congress to use that clause to regulate *intrastate* commerce.

That same year, the Supreme Court considered Congress's taxing scheme in the new Social Security Act, which induced states to establish laws to fund unemployment compensation.[7]

After explaining the plight of unemployment at the time, the hotly divided 5–4 court decision then explained: "the use of the moneys of the nation to relieve the unemployed and their dependents is a use for any purpose narrower than the promotion of the general welfare." [8]

By saying "narrower than the promotion of the general welfare" the Supreme Court meant within the limits of what the Constitution allowed under the "general welfare" clause.

The first part of that quote, however, etches into Supreme Court lore the idea that milk comes from stores. The Court writes about "the use of the moneys of the nation" as if those funds come from some magic savings account conjured by pixie dust. That money is not the nation's. It's yours! And now Congress was getting the green light to spend it at will.

The Supreme Court decided that Congress has unrestricted power to spend, which is limited only by the requirement that the money be used for the "general welfare" of the United States. [9] Well, it seems like virtually every expenditure could be argued as being for the "general welfare" of our country.

Imagine your spouse or other family member saying: "Hey, honey, I'm going to the mall to spend a million dollars, but don't worry, it's for our general welfare." Such whimsy is exactly how Congress has treated the Spending Clause ever since the 1930s.

When the going got tough, Congress and the Supreme Court concluded that it was easier rewriting the law than complying with it.

In the 1970s, Don McLean's song "American Pie" was a huge hit, with its catchy refrain mentioning "the day the music died."

That's what the 1930s was to the Constitution. It was the decade the rule of law died in America.

The fourth Congress understood it had no authority to spend

money to rebuild Savannah. But in recent history, Congress showed no restraint by spending $750 billion to bail out failing banks during the financial crisis of 2008.

Today, Congress considers the Spending Clause to be a blank check. Like the president, the legislative branch of government also has a pen—and uses it often.

UNBALANCED

In fiscal year 2015, the federal government spent $3.69 trillion.[10] That's a lot of groceries.

Where is all that money spent? Almost half of it is for Medicare, Medicaid, Social Security, and related entitlement programs. National defense receives about 18 percent. Eleven percent goes to social welfare programs. Seven percent is required to pay the interest on the nation's skyrocketing debt.[11]

On the revenue side, the United States collected about $3.25 trillion in 2015. That staggering sum of your money is still not enough to pay for Congress's spending habits. The United States collected $440 billion less than it spent last year.

You'd think Congress would be embarrassed by failing to practice what every schoolkid knows—you can't spend more than you have. This maxim applies to grocery shopping and should apply to our government, too.

Congress will continue to pile debt on top of debt and expand government programs and promises even more unless citizens impose meaningful restraints.

My proposed constitutional amendment would compel fiscal discipline for America by requiring Congress to pass a balanced budget every year. Because our national security cannot be compromised, I suggest an exception should exist for war or certain national security issues.

To ensure Congress complies, my plan would automatically freeze federal spending at 90 percent of the preceding year's levels if Congress fails to meet its balanced budget obligations.

Details like this can, and should, be worked out at a convention of states. It's the general agreement to balance our budget that is needed to call for that convention.

My plan also would require Congress to balance its budget by reducing spending rather than by increasing taxes.

Again, details like these are best honed in the crucible of public debate. And I ask you to be part of this debate.

Voices of Doubt

Right about now the doubters chime in. *Amending the Constitution is impossible, and foolish.*

I think we've proven that our debt is foolish, and our solution is sound. But is it possible?

Absolutely.

In 1977, Texas passed an Article V Convention of States proposal for a balanced budget amendment. By comparison to today, the demand in 1977 seems like a trifle. An early draft of the 1977 House Concurrent Resolution began:

> WHEREAS, The unbridled constitutional power of Congress "to borrow money on the credit of the United States" has resulted in almost perennial deficit spending and the steady

growth of a national debt to a dangerous level, estimated to be $617.5 billion at the end of fiscal year 1976.

You've heard the expression *The more things change, the more they stay the same*. In the case of our nation's debt, *the more things stay the same, the worse things get*.

Our annual *interest payment* on America's debt today is almost half the *total debt* when Texas first called for a convention to stop the red ink. Also note the words used in 1977 mimic the recurring complaint we have today: "perennial deficit spending and the steady growth of a national debt to a dangerous level."

Americans' concern hasn't changed. Congress's spending habits haven't changed. The only thing that's changed is the size of the pile of our debt.

Because Congress won't balance its books, it's time for citizens to shut down America's charge account.

We are so close to making this happen.

Recently we were just two states shy of the thirty-four needed to call a convention of states to consider a balanced budget amendment. We need to reassemble the team and add two more states. That's doable. It is necessary.

To paraphrase the late Bum Phillips, famed coach of the Houston Oilers, after a second consecutive failure to reach the Super Bowl: *Decades ago, we knocked on the door. In recent years, we beat on the door. Now it's time to kick the door in!*

We've tried to get Congress to rein in spending. We're tired of their stall tactics. It's time to kick the door in.

Running Together

I suppose that the priorities we hold in our family have helped us stay pretty balanced in life. Our daughter, volunteer causes, and long-time friendships keep us sane in an often insane political world.

Our decision to run for governor was a big one and put us squarely in the fishbowl of public opinion. There was a higher level of pressure in the campaign. Texas is a large state and boasts the twelfth-largest economy in the world.

Audrey was a senior in high school. People had talked to me about running for other offices before, and I'd always said no. The predominant factor was our desire to spend time with our daughter. With Audrey more active in extracurricular activities, and preparing for college, the time was right to run.

This was an attorney general campaign times fifty. The number of presentations, locations, interviews, not to mention the national media were relentless. The scrutiny in my race for governor was even greater because the national spotlight was on it. My opponent established a national and international profile, with support from all fifty states.

When the campaigns get nasty, Cecilia and Audrey feel it and want to protect me. I try to remind them, and remind myself, "Half the people are going to love me, and half are going to hate me. That's just the way it is."

In November 2014, I received more votes than anybody has ever received for governor in the history of Texas.

A few days later, I called a meeting with my staff, many of whom had been with me for many years.

Just as I had as a newly elected attorney general, I explained my vision as governor.

"Our number-one priority as public servants is to follow the law. In the governor's office, that's what we're going to do. We're going to figure out what the law is, and we're going to follow it. In everything you do, this is our lens: 'What is the law, and how do we follow it?'"

I've been told that this type of leadership isn't the norm. I mean, I wasn't making a campaign speech. These people were my close friends and allies. But my words weren't a surprise to them.

"If you have any question about what's legal or what's illegal, if anything that you encounter is in a gray area, stop what you're doing, go talk to a lawyer, figure it out. Make sure you get it right."

Because of this simple mandate, my staff could clearly and confidently make decisions and lead their departments. For my team and me, Follow the Law is a way of life, and a way to ignore the pressures of politics, polls, money, and lobbying. We have our marching orders. When you do the right thing for the right reason, everything else takes care of itself.

Leadership matters. The ripple effect of leadership, good or bad, is enormous.

GOVERNMENTS AND GROCERIES

Why is Congress so frivolous with your money?

Our nation's debt, and its spending, impact you and your pocketbook. Congress's spending spree will be felt by you and me.

When I was a kid, my parents would "splurge" on Christmas spending, ensuring there were always presents under the tree. For my family, it wasn't much. I would typically get a toy or two, plus a needed pair of tennis shoes and a shirt.

To increase the pile under the tree, my mom would always add a gag gift like wrapping up a rock or whatever she could find. She would also often include an item she made herself.

To be honest, though, the best part of Christmas was the meal. My mom was a wonderful home-style cook. She would make homemade bread and turkey dressing. She'd baste the turkey and put it in the oven the night before. The entire house smelled like a big warm meal.

And we always made sure the house was well decorated for the season. A nice Christmas tree with ornaments and lights on, and in, the house.

After Christmas, my mom always reminded us that because we had splurged, we needed to cut back on spending for a while.

I wish she was still around to teach Congress how to stop splurging. Their busted budgets affect the cost of bread and milk, and affect whether you have a job to pay for your groceries.

My mom often took me to the grocery store to help her pick out the food. This was back in the old days, when people paid cash for groceries. Debit cards didn't exist and I don't recall seeing credit cards.

If you didn't have enough cash to pay for everything, you simply had to put some items back. There were times I had to return items to the store shelf while my mom continued with the checkout process. Putting items back is embarrassing, but it brings focus on what's really important.

It's time to tell Congress to put some items back, and pay cash.

{*Thirteen*}

Judging Judges

The Court must be living in another world. Day by day, case by case,
it is busy designing a Constitution for a country I do not recognize.

BD. OF CTY. COMM'RS, WABAUNSEE CTY., KAN. V. UMBEHR,

518 U.S. 668, 711 (1996) (SCALIA, J., DISSENTING).

Some people, okay, *many,* criticize the legal profession and the role lawyers play in our society. And in many cases, I'd agree. But I hope we can also agree about the positive, even crucial, role attorneys play in preserving our freedom.

Many of the Founders of our country were lawyers. Of the fifty-six signers of the Declaration of Independence, twenty-five were lawyers. Of the fifty-five Framers of the Constitution, thirty-two were lawyers. Abraham Lincoln was a practicing attorney before he entered public life.[1]

As in any field of work, there may be some in the legal profession who bring discredit. But by a wide margin, lawyers have been part of the fight for the constitutional rights of their fellow Americans. I say "part of" because we must always remember the men and women of our armed forces who have fought, and often made the ultimate sacrifice, for our freedom. They have been, and continue to be, on the literal front lines of this fight. All Americans must work every day to fulfill the promise of the freedom our military has fought to defend.

Since college, my purpose for joining the legal profession was to do precisely what I did as attorney general, and in my current role as governor: use the law as a tool to fight for a greater, orderly society that promotes the common good.

I sought to achieve those lawful goals when I filed each of thirty-four lawsuits against the federal government. I sought to uphold the greatest tool ever created for a free and orderly society—the U.S. Constitution.

But I've also seen firsthand that it takes more than lawsuits to defend the Constitution.

Just look at what happened with Obamacare. We sued to stop it—twice. And twice, the Supreme Court did the legislative work of rewriting the language of Obamacare to save it. The Obamacare law is just one example of all three branches of government circumventing the Constitution.

Part of the genius of the Constitution is that its authors gave us a tool kit to restore the rule of law when it gets broken.

POP QUIZ

Question: How many votes does it take to amend the Constitution?

I ask that question at speeches, and the answer I hear most often is "two-thirds." Sometimes I'll hear people say, "three-fourths."

To some extent both answers have a sense of accuracy.

It takes two-thirds of the House and Senate to agree to a proposed amendment, or, two-thirds of the states must agree to call a convention to propose amendments. But that's just the starting point.

After an amendment is proposed—whether by Congress or a convention of states—three-fourths of the states must ratify the amendment before it becomes part of the Constitution.

But that's just what the Constitution says. And as you know by now, what the Constitution says and how it's applied are often far different.

The real answer to the pop quiz question is "five."

The Constitution is changed almost every year with just five votes of Supreme Court justices in hotly divided cases. (It takes just five of the nine justices to decide a case.)

Remember that the Constitution begins with "We the People." It was written by the people and for the people, with most of the power in this country remaining with the people.

So how in the world do five unelected and unaccountable lawyers on the Supreme Court have the power to speak for the people? And the power to change the people's governing document?

They don't! But, nevertheless, it happens virtually every year.

Earlier chapters have exposed the Supreme Court for what it has become. It has abandoned its intended role of "calling balls and strikes" and has assumed the mantle of a super-legislature that makes up laws or rewrites them at will.

Even worse, it has assumed the authority to single-handedly amend the Constitution without giving the people of this country any say in the process.

The Congress that crafted the Bill of Rights began their next session by invoking God. From the time of George Washington until the late 1900s, God was openly invoked by presidents and government officials at all levels.

But that didn't deter new-era Supreme Court justices from *knowing* far better what the Constitution provides. Now, they increasingly side with the anti-God crowd.

The Supreme Court is so cavalier that it even ruled differently on the same day about Ten Commandment displays by government bodies. Rather than the First Amendment providing a rule of law, the Court is applying it as a rule of whim.

The Supreme Court showed similar caprice for the Tenth Amendment. In 1976, the Court ruled that under the Tenth Amendment the federal government can't dictate to state and local governments how much they pay their employees.

Nine years later, the Court overturned that very decision and concluded the very opposite. The Constitution hadn't changed. A Supreme Court justice changed his mind.

When the Constitution was written, administrative agencies like the EPA weren't considered to be part of government; and most certainly unaccountable administrative agencies were not authorized by the Constitution to write and adjudicate the laws we live under. That's largely the way the Constitution was applied for well over a century.

In 1935, the Supreme Court held that "Congress is not permitted to abdicate or to transfer to others the essential legislative functions." A few years later the Supreme Court turned on a dime and suddenly decided that allowing unelected, unaccountable bureaucrats to make and enforce law was a fabulous idea.

After the Court reconstructed the Constitution, administrative agencies have now grown to the extent that they make more than 90 percent of the federal laws and rules that govern your lives. Did you—the People—have any say in that constitutional change? Not a bit!

But the Supreme Court didn't stop there. During that same short period in the 1930s, the Supreme Court rewrote the Commerce Clause.

In 1935, the Court ruled that Congress didn't have the power to regulate *intra*state commerce. Just two years later, the Court changed its mind and has since allowed Congress to regulate virtually everything. So much for America being a nation of law rather than of men.

During that very same time period the Supreme Court abandoned previous rulings that limited Congress's spending ability. That decision and later expansions of that decision have empowered Congress to dig us into a $19 trillion debt.

You—and our nation—are paying the price for a Supreme Court that has come untethered from the Constitution and is now deciding cases on the basis of personal beliefs rather than on constitutional principles.

Contrary to the power it has assumed, the Supreme Court has no power to make the law or to establish policy. Judges were never given the power to determine what the law *should* be. Instead they have the power to say only what the law is as it applies to a particular case.

The Americans who ratified the Constitution understood that the judiciary "can take no active resolution whatsoever." It was clear from the beginning that courts "have neither force nor will, but merely judgment."[2]

Because of the courts' limited ability to shape society, they were considered by the Founders to be "the least dangerous to the political rights of the Constitution." Oops!

The Supreme Court in recent decades has changed from its intended role and has now become the most dangerous branch of government. Why? Because they can change any law and are accountable to no one.

LIVING AND BREATHING?

Let's talk about another viewpoint, those who assert the Constitution is intended to be "a living, breathing document" that continually changes.

If this is true, who determines how it changes?

The knee-jerk answer: the United States Supreme Court. But why do five unelected, unaccountable lawyers who wear black robes have unrestrained power to alter the social and economic rules of this country? This conclusion is found nowhere in the Constitution.

Our judicial branch of government was never intended to have the level of power they assert today. Instead, the democratic process of the people was intended to run this country.

This is one reason for this book, and the constitutional amendments I propose. We must restore to the people the power to govern their lives.

Instead of allowing the unaccountable Supreme Court to fabricate a "living, breathing Constitution," on their own terms, I prefer a living and breathing citizenry, empowering their states, to follow the carefully framed owner's manual found in Article V.

THE PROBLEM WITH THE JUDICIARY

The operation was a success, but the patient died. What such a procedure is to medicine, the Court's opinion in this case is to law.

NATIONAL ENDOWMENT FOR THE ARTS V. FINLEY,

524 U.S. 569 (1998) (SCALIA, J., CONCURRING)

The Founders intended the judiciary to police the separation of powers among the three branches of government.[3]

During the early decades of our nation the courts fulfilled that duty.[4]

As Alexander Hamilton explained, "the courts were designed to be an intermediate body between the people and the legislature, in order, among other things, to keep the latter within the limits assigned to their authority."[5]

Today, courts have abandoned that fundamental duty. Courts are no longer behaving like courts.[6]

The Supreme Court has sailed far from its intended limited role and has begun asserting the legislative power it was supposed to police. Instead of applying the rules, made by the legislators you elected, the Supreme Court is making the rules and "amending" the Constitution itself without giving you a right to ratify or reject the amendments.

In the cloistered halls of the Supreme Court, America's original design is constantly being redesigned. Americans infused into our Declaration of Independence the right to chart our own liberty. That right was secured in the Constitution. Your freedom is now under assault by the whims and personal beliefs of five lawyers in robes.

Why waste the time, money, and effort to galvanize fellow Americans to your point of view to amend the Constitution when all you have to do is win over five judges on the Supreme Court?

Social change happens, and the Constitution can change with it. That's the way democracy works. But democracy doesn't work by judicial fiat!

The Eighteenth and Twenty-First Amendments show how the Constitution was designed to work. The Eighteenth imposed Prohibition, the Twenty-First repealed it just more than a decade later. The citizens of America were able to amend the Constitution to abide by the collective attitudes of Americans at the time.

Lately, citizens with a grievance have been able to bypass that process and ignore the lawful procedure to amend the Constitution in Article V because the Supreme Court has assumed the authority to freely "amend" the Constitution itself. Rather than citizens engaging millions of Americans to determine the will of the people, just five lawyers can impose their will on the citizens.

The people of America are now subjects of the Lord Masters who sit on the Supreme Court. The Constitution's authors would have soundly rejected this design.

The late Justice Scalia openly lamented the Supreme Court's errant ways: "The Court must be living in another world. Day by day, case by case, it is busy designing a Constitution for a country I do not recognize." [7]

Everyone who hails Supreme Court justices who depart from the Constitution and rely on the "living and breathing" constitutional concept to apply their own personal beliefs should be forewarned. The precedent is set to overturn those decisions based on the personal preferences of future justices. In other words, be careful what you wish for.

My Proposal

Because the Supreme Court has strayed so far for so long from its intended role, it is time that the citizens of America—the people who are intended to run this country—assert accountability on the Court. The Founders gave us the ability to fix problems like this with tools like Article V in the Constitution.

The Constitution is a document where people relinquished control of some of their lives to a government, under the condition that the government control itself. The people who live under the Constitution have the inherent right to rein in any branch of government that exceeds its authority. This is precisely what Article V of the Constitution authorizes you to do.

I propose that the Article V process be used to allow a supermajority of states to overturn a Supreme Court decision when the decision goes beyond deciding a case among parties and establishes a new constitutional right or obligation that applies to all Americans.

Because that decision would ipso facto be an amendment to the Constitution, the people—through the states—should have a say in whether it will be accepted or rejected. In keeping with the Article V process, it should require the vote of two-thirds of the states to call for a convention and three-fourths of the states to agree to overturn a court decision.

Because an Article V convention of states can be convened around a single issue, the process can be focused, and relatively swift. (*Swift*, in the governmental sense of the word.)

When the ink dried on the Constitution in 1787, no one intended for the Supreme Court to have power to unilaterally amend the Constitution and to act as a super-legislature. It's time that the people who live under that Constitution force the Supreme Court to abide by it the way it was intended.

THE VOICE OF THE STATES

To some people, even the thought of Americans coming together to overturn a Supreme Court decision may seem disorienting or dangerous. To those, I ask, "Do you really want five unelected lawyers, who can't be fired, to impose their personal bias on you and your family?"

As I wrote in my paper *Restoring the Rule of Law*: "The Framers were deliberate in vesting the people (and their closest representatives, namely, the state legislatures) with the power to amend the Constitution. The people have been robbed of that authority if the Supreme Court can change what the Constitution means with the stroke of a pen."

My proposed amendments restore the people's control over their Constitution by giving states the power to fix errant Supreme Court decisions.[8]

The internal rule created by the Supreme Court to decide cases by a razor-thin five-to-four majority may be well and fine when it comes to deciding a case between two parties. But such a close margin of five liberal lawyers is unacceptable when it comes to using court decisions to amend or rewrite the Constitution.

If the Constitution is going to be altered by the Supreme Court, the justices should meet the same supermajority hurdle required for the United States to amend the Constitution.

Under Article V, three-fourths of the states are required to ratify an amendment. That supermajority requirement was intended to ensure the document isn't shredded by the whims of the day or by the rule of a bare majority.

But the Founders had no idea that the whims of the day would be imposed by Supreme Court justices. After all, they were considered by the Founders to be the most harmless branch to our liberty.

I propose requiring the Supreme Court to have three-fourths of its members to agree on any decision that alters the Constitution in a way that expands or contracts the rights or obligations of American citizens.

That would mean that seven of the nine justices must agree before they rewrite the Constitution.

INTENDED CONSEQUENCES

This higher threshold for the Supreme Court would have the additional benefit of forcing more constitutional amendment proposals through the democratic process where they belong. If the Constitution is going to be amended, it should be in the open, with all Americans having an opportunity to weigh in.

I would also suggest that the seven-justice supermajority vote requirement be applied to Supreme Court decisions that strike down democratically enacted laws.

Laws, whether they be passed by Congress or your state legislature, reflect the voice of you and your fellow citizens. If you don't like a law, you can complain to your representative about it and even try to defeat that representative.

But once a law is in place, it represents the collective wisdom and judgment of the people. For the United States, a law is representative of more than 300 million people. A state law in Texas is representative of more than 27 million people.

So why is it that five lawyers, none of whom are from Texas (and probably not from your state, either), can invalidate a state law, without any accountability?

Remember, the Founders constructed the Constitution to foster democracy, not crush it. By deviating from the Founders' intent and allowing five lawyers to overturn a democratically developed law, the will of the people is thwarted, not advanced.

WILL THE SKY FALL?

I've actually had some naysayers protest, "What if some crazy state passes a law imposing slavery?" Remember, the Constitution trumps federal and state laws. The Constitution prohibits slavery.

The Bill of Rights, and the additional amendments, exist to protect you from federal and state governments passing laws contrary to your inalienable rights. That's why I'm still in awe of the Constitution, and hope that you are, too.

Think the notion of requiring seven of nine Supreme Court justices is too novel or untested?

To the contrary, the supermajority requirement has long been used in our legal system. For example, the federal government and every state already require a supermajority (and sometimes unanimity) of votes to convict someone of a serious crime.

There are reasons for this supermajority requirement in criminal cases. Taking a person's liberty and property is the ultimate act by government. Before we do that we want to eliminate the risk that a simple majority of decision makers would get the answer wrong.

The same theory applies to the Supreme Court altering the Constitution or invalidating a democratically enacted law with a razor-thin margin. When doing so, the Court is often compromising someone's liberty, property, or other fundamental rights.

To make sure Supreme Court justices don't get it wrong, to ensure the result is based on valid legal reasoning rather than their increasingly evident personal biases, a three-fourths supermajority should be required before the Supreme Court can trump the democratic process or rewrite the Constitution. This simply imposes on the Supreme Court the high standards established by the Founders in Article V of the Constitution.

Importantly, this is not uncharted territory. The supermajority requirement is already used by courts in states like Nebraska and North Dakota. This process can work equally as well at the United States Supreme Court.[9]

THE SOLUTION: ALLOW A SUPERMAJORITY OF STATES TO OVERRULE

My proposals prune the three branches of government to the structure intended by the Founders.

In America, the People are at the apex, with government under them. To retain that framework and to promote democracy, the people themselves must have a voice in how their government operates and a say in the rules that govern their lives.

For example, the legislative and executive branches of government are directly accountable to the people. If they do something wrong, voters can impose change by electing a new president or new members to Congress who can chart a course consistent with the will of the people.

If the Supreme Court veers off course, however, there is no corrective device. The people have no say, because the justices aren't accountable to them. The justices serve for life, and many serve during the stretch of three or four presidents.

Everyone understands the need for an independent judiciary, but as the system exists now, Supreme Court justices can—and have—single-handedly rewritten the Constitution.

I don't know what kind of government that is, but it's not democracy.

Thomas Jefferson had a word for it. He wrote that giving "judges the right to decide what laws are constitutional, and what not, not only for themselves in their own sphere of action, but for the Legislature and Executive also, in their spheres, would make the judiciary a despotic branch." [10]

How right he was.

The Founders had no idea the judicial branch of government could so far deviate from the carefully crafted Constitution. They did foresee, however, that we would need tools to rein in a runaway branch of government.

The Founders set ground rules for our fledgling nation. They also established consequences for breaking those rules by giving us Article V to correct misbehavior by government as our nation grew. Failure by the people to enforce those ground rules leads to further misbehavior and eventually to chaos.

We should heed the Founders' advice and use the tools they gave us.

LONG-TERM BENEFITS

When Audrey was a young teenager, we set ground rules for use of her cell phone and the Internet. One time she broke those rules. By a two-thirds supermajority vote, Cecilia and I took her cell phone and computer away for an entire week.

You would have thought we had imposed cruel and unusual punishment. The crying seemed to never end. As the saying goes, that week was the longest year of my life.

I remembered my parents saying, when they were about to impose discipline for some misdeed: "This is going to hurt me a lot more than it will you." *Yeah, right,* I thought.

As a parent I realized how correct they were. Sometimes it's hard for parents to discipline their children. We don't ever want to see our kids sad or angry.

But more important, we don't want our children straying into areas of chronic misbehavior. We know that one stray act compounded on another can lead to a chaotic life.

The same principle applies to people as a group. We the People recognized that we needed certain rules if we were going to form a compact of self-governance. We wrote those rules in the Constitution.

When those rules are followed, the citizens have a sense of certainty and the security that comes with it. From the Constitution flows a sense of order for our society that has elevated our form of government above others.

Yes, there were tears at times. Remember the wailing when Congress refused to bail out a burned-out Savannah? Congress knew it was a tough decision, but also knew it was the constitutionally correct decision for the long-term benefit of the entire nation.

And yes, there were times when America needed to change the rules. Slavery is the most obvious example. But rather than changing the rules by judicial fiat, the country changed them the way the Founders designed—by constitutional amendments.

Allowing Supreme Court justices to rewrite the law is like allowing teenagers to make up the rules they live under. It doesn't take long for things to become chaotic.

How We Respond to Challenges

No matter how hard life gets, never give up on your dreams.
—AUDREY ABBOTT

Most Americans know a thing or two about overcoming challenges.

With the help of my family, wonderful medical professionals, and the grace of God, I overcame unimaginable adversity.

I've also overcome challenges imposed by government. Contrary to many political prognosticators—and even legal scholars—my experience as a judge, Texas attorney general, and governor has shown we can fight—and win—battles to restore our country's freedom and order.

America doesn't need more theory or think tanks. You and I are ready for action.

I've been on the political battlefield in historic legal fights that have refined and strengthened the Constitution. We can fix our broken government, and solidify the freedom we were created to enjoy.

Sounds impossible—especially after an evening of watching cable news. But in this book, I hope you've seen a few glimpses of the impossible becoming possible.

On January 20, 2015, I was sworn in as governor of the second-largest state in America. Thirty years earlier, I lay in a hospital bed with a broken back.

Would I ever walk? Could Cecilia and I have a child? Would I even be able to work? Was my law career over before it began?

I am living proof that we live in a country where a young man's life can literally be broken in half and yet he can still rise up and become governor of his state and have a great family.

POSSIBILITIES

Can I tell you the reasons I wrote this book?

I want you to believe in possibilities for your life. If a guy in a wheelchair, with a broken back, can take consistent steps to move forward in his life, you can, too.

I want future generations to enjoy freedom, prosperity, and possibility.

We must constantly reimagine possibilities for our lives, our families, our careers—and our country.

It's possible for each of us to succeed because of the freedoms we enjoy in America.

It's possible to follow constitutional principles that fortify freedom in our lives.

It's possible to win elections based on our nation's foundational principles.

It's possible to fix the fractures in our constitutional foundation.

Impossible?

As governor I can recognize, as never before, the powers and potential excesses of executive office. But I've seen that it's not only possible to govern based on foundational principles—it's essential.

My life was broken, but I remained unbowed. I fought through the pain because I believed restoration was possible. I fight to fix a broken government because I believe in a better future for the United States—it's in our DNA.

This same fight is found in the DNA of Americans across the country. We've all experienced some level of brokenness and challenge. Right now, there are Americans battling against cancer. There are single moms working two jobs to feed and educate their children so they can have a brighter future. Every day, despite the odds, entrepreneurs launch new businesses and create jobs in their communities.

You and I are heirs to an American legacy of conquering challenges.

It started with the Declaration of Independence and our fight for freedom. We stood up to oppression in World War II and found our resilience after September 11, 2001. Throughout our unmatched history, the people of this great land have remained unbowed in the face of daunting circumstances.

We've never backed down from a fight. Instead, the righteousness of our cause has emboldened us to act.

WE FACE TOUGH CHALLENGES ONCE AGAIN

Today, we must fight against our own federal government.

Our government has fostered a culture of duplicity, stirred up by the very people charged to lead us and protect us.

We were told that ISIS was "the J.V. team" and "contained," only to watch their evil spread around the globe, and even into our own country.

The federal government charged with securing our border has been accused by a federal judge of conspiring to help people enter the country illegally. And they are coming by the thousands each week.

Americans were told, "If you like your doctor, you can keep your doctor."

We're supposed to believe the attack on the U.S. consulate in Benghazi was a reaction to a video, and trust that the IRS makes decisions free from any political calculations.

Leaders in Washington, D.C., keep trying to convince us that guns, not criminals, are the cause of crime.

We've been told the very best U.S. intelligence agencies, such as the FBI and Department of Homeland Security, don't have the ability to vet people coming from terrorist-infused cultures. And yet, states are forced to accept refugees from those countries who then turn around and try to blow up our cities.

In short, we're told to trust—despite a steady stream of insulting lies.

To add insult to injury, when citizens raise concerns about falsehoods like these, we are given sanctimonious lectures that appeal to a globalization that is far different from the American exceptionalism we've worked so hard to achieve.

We've had enough of falsehoods and incompetence from

officials—elected and unelected—who have abandoned the first principle of the Constitution: government exists to serve the citizens.

Possible

We've shown that it is possible to rein in the federal government when the people show the backbone needed to do so.

You may have heard the saying *America did not create religious liberty. Religious liberty created America*. I agree. That's why I've fought for religious freedom, and prevailed, all the way to the United States Supreme Court.

When the ACLU fought to remove the words "under God" from Barack Obama's inaugural oath of office, we fought, and those words were recited.

When pro-abortion groups tried to overturn a ban on partial-birth abortion, we responded, and we won.

When the EPA exceeded its regulatory authority, we fought them, and we won.

When the United States, the United Nations, and the International Court of Justice tried to force Texas to forsake our sovereignty in deciding how to punish a criminal from another country, we stood our ground, and we won.

When the president used his pen to make immigration "law," we stood up against his lawlessness and put a halt to his executive excess.

Texas hasn't patented a system for governing or for "freedom." We only insist on abiding by the genius of the Founders.

ON THE BRINK

But take it from me—it takes more than lawsuits to fix what's broken in Washington, D.C. Just look at what happened with Obamacare.

We sued to stop it—twice. And twice the Supreme Court rewrote the language of the Obamacare law to save it. In doing so, the judicial branch of government abandoned its duty to police the other branches and assumed the legislative role.

The president went even further. He altered Obamacare more than thirty times without approval of Congress. The executive branch of government has usurped the legislative branch's authority to make the law.

Unfortunately, the problems don't stop there.

With each religious liberty case we win, others are lost that set back the historical recognition of God in America.

With each victory against the EPA, or some other federal agency, there are many more cases where the Supreme Court expands administrative agencies' power to rule over you.

With each attempt to enforce the Tenth Amendment, there are countless rulings that crush it.

With every ruling that appears to uphold the Constitution, there are too many that rewrite our foundational document.

And it just got worse.

As I wrote this, the fiercest fighter for freedom on the U.S. Supreme Court had just passed away. Justice Scalia was more than a jurist; he was a true constitutionalist. He believed in the power of the Constitution and the necessity of applying it rather than rewriting it.

We are now at a constitutional tipping point in America. With a solid bloc of four liberal justices already on the Supreme Court, one more liberal justice replacing Antonin Scalia would provide the majority-clinching vote needed to impose radical constitutional transformations like what occurred in the 1930s.

Principles that we've taken for granted are on the brink of elimination.

The decision upholding the Ten Commandments was 5–4, with Scalia voting in favor.

The decision to uphold the individual right to keep and bear arms under the Second Amendment was 5–4, with Scalia writing the opinion.

The Court's decision to temporarily block the EPA's multibillion-dollar hijacking of America's power sector occurred several days before Justice Scalia's death and was a 5–4 ruling, with Scalia voting in favor.

That matter will now go through the full litigation process and return to the Supreme Court without Justice Scalia. The new justice may be the tiebreaking vote on whether the EPA is allowed to expand its tentacles or if it is reined in.

Two cases currently at the Supreme Court from Texas will decide the social and legal landscape for an entire generation. One involves the president's executive order granting amnesty to millions of people in the country illegally. The other involves abortion.

Those cases will be decided after this book is published and after Justice Scalia's death. Based on Justice Scalia's past decisions, it's fair to conclude that the scales of justice will substantially shift in those cases if he is replaced with a liberal justice.

Justice Scalia would never let a president get away with rewriting immigration laws. If the four liberal justices on the Court are joined by a like-minded jurist who fills Scalia's seat, the keys to the congressional vault will be handed to the president.

WHAT WE CAN DO TOGETHER

The future of this country is too important to place its helm in the hands of one unaccountable jurist on the Supreme Court. And, as we've seen, the other branches of government have strayed from their mission.

There comes a time when we—as a people—must come together and decide our fate. Now is that time.

America is not only *for* the people; we're a nation *by* the people. It's our collective responsibility.

When we outsource our responsibility as citizens, we're going to be disappointed every time. We need to face the fact that newly elected officials, new laws, and new court rulings will not fix what's broken. They are the cause of the problem. Citizens are the solution.

The vision and plan, outlined in this book, come down to this: We need to fix our country's broken foundation. We need to repair the damage done to the Constitution by all three government branches. The task may seem daunting, but it's definitely doable.

The fix will not come from Washington, D.C. Instead, the states must unite and lead the way. And when I say *states* I'm talking about you, me, our friends, our neighbors, and our state legislators.

The good news is that we have a head start. There are several national programs focused on the issue, and many states have already passed measures to begin the process or are considering them.

In January 2016, I joined the effort by outlining my plan, titled *Restoring the Rule of Law, with States Leading the Way.* The proposal consists of nine amendments to the Constitution that will restore the rule of law in America.

PRUNING BRANCHES

Because all three branches of government have strayed from the Constitution, we can probably agree that the federal government cannot be trusted to correct itself.

Right?

Amazingly, more than two hundred years ago, the Framers of the Constitution foresaw this possibility. Their solution? The people of America, through their state legislatures, must bring correction.

Article V of the Constitution provides the clear path the Founders intended for lawful change. The Founders empowered states to call a convention to propose specific amendments to the Constitution to adjust for the times or correct errant government actions.

The path involves state legislatures passing a proposal to participate in a convention, and deciding which proposals should be considered. My recommendation is that the authorization be limited to a few specific propositions, and limited in time.

Placing an expiration date on the states' authority to participate in a convention to consider amendments is important to ensure that the convention relates only to the pressing issues of the day. I suggest that you don't want to grant open-ended authority for a convention of states that could occur thirty or fifty years from now when the political dynamics may have changed.

For example, I would propose the State of Texas be authorized to participate in a convention of states to consider the amendments to the U.S. Constitution listed below. The authority for Texas to participate in any such convention should expire ten years after the authority is given. For Texas to participate in a convention of states after this period, new authorization would be required. I suggest each state have similar time restraints.

There are several "fixes" to consider for a convention of states that I've proposed in this book and several more that I outlined in my *Restoring the Rule of Law* plan.

To correct an executive branch that has exceeded its intended constitutional role, I propose:

- Prohibit administrative agencies—and the unelected bureaucrats who staff them—from creating federal law.
- Prohibit administrative agencies—and the unelected bureaucrats who staff them—from preempting state law.

To restore the power that states and citizens were intended to have to check an overreaching federal government, I propose the following amendments to put teeth into the Tenth Amendment and to protect state sovereignty:

- Amend the Tenth Amendment by clarifying that all powers not *"expressly"* delegated to the federal government in the Constitution remain with the states and the people.
- Amend the Tenth Amendment to give states the power to sue the federal government when it oversteps its bounds.
- Allow a two-thirds majority of the states to override a federal law or regulation.

To prevent Congress from regulating where it shouldn't and to force it to regulate itself:

- Prohibit Congress from regulating activity that occurs only within one state. This prevents Congress from using the Commerce Clause to overregulate.
- Require Congress to balance its budget.

To balance the scales of the judiciary:

- Allow a three-fourths majority of the states to override a U.S. Supreme Court decision.
- Require a seven-justice supermajority vote by U.S. Supreme Court justices for decisions that amend the Constitution by creating new constitutional rights or obligations or decisions that invalidate a democratically enacted law.

Let's consider these a starting point for a discussion that needs to begin.

These fixes are based on "cracks" I've seen in the Constitution, and my experience challenging the federal government's abuse of power.

You may agree, or disagree, with some or all of my proposals. You may have other specific ideas. But we can all agree there's a need for a lawful solution, because the freedoms upon which our country was founded are slowly, but surely, being eroded and something must be done about it.

Sitting on the sidelines is no longer an option.

You and your friends have more say in shaping your government and our nation than you've been led to believe. You've been given the power and the tools to do something about it.

All you need to do is convince your state representatives that the time for change is now. Use that email list you have; take to Twitter and Facebook; tell your contacts that it's time to take the Constitution back from a federal government that has grown increasingly disdainful of you and your concerns.

RADICAL AND SCARY

Some people, especially liberals, impulsively denounce convention-of-states efforts that would allow citizens to take control of their government. For example, on the day I outlined my plan to amend the Constitution, the liberal American Civil Liberties Union of Texas issued a statement saying: "Governor Abbott, as Texans, we prefer the Framers' plan. Don't mess with the Constitution." [1]

This statement reveals common mistakes by critics of states and citizens working to fix what the liberals helped break.

First, they say they "prefer the Framers' plan." Great! So do I. The apparent difference is that I know what the ACLU ignores: the Framers' plan included the Article V process I'm calling for.

Second, they demand: "Don't mess with the Constitution." Perhaps they are unaware that the Founders themselves "messed" with the Constitution. Two years after the Constitution was written, the Founders proposed dozens of amendments to fix flaws in the original Constitution of 1787. Ten of them became the Bill of Rights; and the Eleventh and Twelfth Amendments were added just a few years later.

The Founders told us, and showed us, their intent was for the Constitution to be amended.

At heart, liberals love to amend the Constitution. They just prefer doing it the modern way by using liberal judges to do the work rather than citizens using the Article V process intended by the Founders.

As usual, the people who are most against an Article V solution are the ones who benefit most from inaction—and have the most to lose from our action.

Personally, I trust the American people more than I trust the federal government.

Other concerns are equally unfounded. Neither an overhaul of the Constitution nor radical alterations of it are possible. A convention of states is intended only for *amendments* to the existing Constitution, not a complete rewriting of it. Moreover, because no amendment would be effective unless three-fourths of the states (38 of them) agreed, absurd proposals feared by some critics would never stand a chance of passing.

A better authority for the right approach is Antonin Scalia himself.

On the propriety of a convention of states, Scalia said:

> The founders inserted this alternative method of obtaining constitutional amendments because they knew the Congress would be unwilling to give attention to many issues the people are concerned with, particularly those involving restrictions on the federal government's own power. The founders foresaw that and they provided the convention as a remedy. If the only way to get that convention is to take this minimal risk, then it is a reasonable one.[2]

Scalia expressed frustrations similar to what Americans feel today, and the challenges discussed in this book:

> I am not sure how long a people can accommodate to directives from a legislature it feels is no longer responsive, and to direc-

tives from a life-tenured judiciary that was never meant to be responsive, without losing its will to control its own destiny.[3]

Scalia elaborated on why it should be the people and the states who propose amendments rather than Congress:

Congress knows that the people want more fiscal responsibility, but it is unwilling to oblige it. . . . If the only way to clarify the law, if the only way to remove us from utter bondage to the Congress, is to take what I think to be a minimal risk on this limited convention, then let's take it.[4]

Let's not lose our will to control our own destiny as Scalia warned. Let's take his advice about a limited convention to free us from the bondage of the federal government.

WHICH WOULD YOU CHOOSE?

Many pundits seem to have a knee-jerk reaction to the idea of a convention of states. (If you don't believe me, give this book to a friend, or bring up the subject in your next conversation about politics.) But let's stop being entangled in theories and arguments.

Which is worse for our country: a convention where a supermajority of states discuss the rightful powers of the federal government— or a president, Congress, and thousands of unelected bureaucrats dismissively ignoring the Constitution?

My proposals ensure we remain a nation under the rule of law, rather than the rule of men. The amendments allow us to live up to our promise of greater opportunity for every citizen.

Your state, our country, the future our children inherit, will be defined by how we respond to the challenges we face.

We must stand up to the challenge, one more time, before it's too late.

Freedom

Like many Texas families, mine is multicultural by choice. My family gatherings include the Segura, Cuellar, Rocha, Torres, Gamez, and Valdillez families. We share more than a meal—we share conservative values.

Conservative is not a color, a race, or an ethnicity. It is a commitment to the ideal that every American has a chance to succeed; that faith and family are foremost; that jobs and education are the best pathways to a better future. We believe in freedom.

Free countries need a free marketplace. The cornerstone of a healthy economy is an environment where every American has the freedom to aspire, to innovate, to risk, and to prosper.

Increasingly, government is a hindrance, rather than a help, to economic growth. The flood of new regulations limits the ability of workers to take home more pay.

When government is limited, freedom is expanded. When freedom is extended, free enterprise flourishes and individuals prosper.

Fifty years ago, Detroit was described in glowing terms, which sound like descriptions of the Texas economy today. Believe it or not, Detroit was one of the fastest-growing and most prosperous cities in America. But after an era of big-government "help" and increased spending, Detroit spiraled downward into bankruptcy.

Today we see the same poor policy choices begin to choke off opportunity across America. Twenty-five years ago, America's debt was $2.6 trillion. Now our national debt exceeds $19 trillion. Even Greece has less debt per person than America.

Once again, unrestrained growth of government is the cause of these problems. Workers and take-home pay are the victims.

Texas has become the most robust job market in the country because we insist on low taxes, less government, reasonable regulations, and "right to work" laws.

To get America on the right track, we must never forget that you know better how to spend your money than do bureaucrats in Washington, D.C.

These aren't merely the values of a particular political party, or a particular state, they're commonsense values, American values.

YOUR DREAMS

I hope this book has been informative and inspiring. I hope you'll join us in our fight to restore lawful freedom and fix our country's foundation—before it's too late.

But ultimately, this book is about you, your freedom, and your family's future.

Yes, our government is broken, but America is not broken. You, and you alone, are the architect of your future and the co-architect of our country's future. You know how to run your life and career far better than distant and unaccountable rulers in Washington, D.C.

Imagine a country where you, not government, decide what's best for your family.

Do you dream of starting a business and growing it without crushing regulations?

What if we didn't have to watch the news every day, just to keep up with the latest power grabs from our government?

Imagine elected officials and unelected bureaucrats who are committed to you and to the Constitution rather than to their own personal preferences.

America is at a crossroads. We can stand and unite around the rule of law and remain a nation firmly founded on the Constitution, or we can accept our dysfunctional government with a shrug. I'm so glad our country has a history of fighting for freedom.

From Valley Forge to Vicksburg, from the Civil War to Civil Rights, from the Cold War to the War on Terror, Americans have always remembered that freedom is worth fighting for.

America has always risen above our challenges. People like you have taken action with character and courage. In this country, it's the people, not the government, who matter most.

Our future will always remain bright as long as the people respond to the challenge.

I hope my overcoming obstacles can be useful to your life challenges. You have a calling. You have dreams for a better life. There's no reason you can't fulfill those aspirations.

Yes, there will be challenges. No doubt you've experienced your share, and maybe you're in the middle of life-shaking battles. I've been there. Keep moving forward.

I once had a dream of restoring the Constitution and the rule of law in America. That dream was crushed by a falling tree. I learned, however, that even the most daunting obstacles are no reason to give up your dreams. Now, I'm living the dream.

My dreams may have been momentarily broken, but I remained unbowed.

Don't ever give up on your dreams.

AUDREY'S INTRODUCTION

Cecilia and I sometimes have the honor of hearing our daughter introduce me on the campaign trail. It's not very common for teenagers to get up in front of a big crowd and introduce their dad. Frankly, it's not very common for teenagers to even *talk* to their parents.

We are lucky because Audrey loves the campaign trail. Believe it or not, campaigning doesn't have to be all-consuming—or negative. Here's some of what she said at an event last year.

As a teen, I look for role models. I look for leaders who can provide hope and opportunity for my generation. I look for people like my dad.

Daughters love to brag on their dads. And I'm no exception. We still watch Disney movies together. One weekend we watched three seasons of Friday Night Lights *on Netflix. He helped get me ready for softball season. We've gone to countless concerts together. And, like it or not, he still monitors my homework.*

I love my dad. But maybe, more importantly, I admire him. He does more than care for me. He sets an example for me. My dad represents the real meaning of the word courage—*to do what is right no matter how many are against you.*

You can't help but be inspired by my dad when you're around him. He's a reminder that no matter how hard life gets, never give up on your dreams.

ONE MORE TIME

After my accident, during rehab and beyond, I had to rebuild my strength. I spent hours rolling my wheelchair up an eight-story parking garage in Houston. As I pushed up each steep floor, it got harder and harder. But I wouldn't quit until I reached the top. Then back to the bottom for one more climb.

"Just one more," I'd tell myself. "Just one more."

I see life that way. I see bright possibilities for our country that way.

To get to the top, we must push ourselves to do just one more.

I ask that you join me in "just one more" endeavor to fix our country's foundation.

Together we will ensure our lives are not defined by how we're challenged. Instead, they're defined by how we respond to life's challenges.

This applies to America today. It applies to you today.

How We Can Respond Together

Contact your representatives in the State House and State Senate, and ask them to support an Article V convention of states.

Give friends a copy of this book.

If your friends happen to work for the federal government, tell them to buy their own copy of this book. (Just kidding. Give them a copy.)

Go to www.GregAbbott.com/book to find more resources, subscribe to our email list, and follow us on social media.

Appendix A:

Cornhusker Kickback Letter

December 30, 2009

The Honorable Nancy Pelosi
Speaker, United States House of Representatives
Washington, DC 20515

The Honorable Harry Reid
Majority Leader, United States Senate
Washington, DC 20510

The undersigned state attorneys general, in response to numerous inquiries, write to express our grave concern with the Senate version of the Patient Protection and Affordable Care Act ("H.R. 3590"). The current iteration of the bill contains a provision that affords special treatment to the state of Nebraska under the federal Medicaid program. We believe this provision is constitutionally flawed. As chief legal officers of our states we are contemplating a legal challenge to this provision and we ask you to take action to render this challenge unnecessary by striking that provision.

It has been reported that Nebraska Senator Ben Nelson's vote, for H.R. 3590, was secured only after striking a deal that the federal government would bear the cost of newly eligible Nebraska Medicaid enrollees. In marked contrast all other states would not be similarly treated, and instead would be required to allocate substantial sums, potentially totaling billions of dollars, to accommodate H.R. 3590's new Medicaid mandates. In addition to violating the most basic and universally held notions of what is fair and just, we also believe this provision of H.R. 3590 is inconsistent with protections afforded by the United States Constitution against arbitrary legislation.

In *Helvering v. Davis*, 301 U.S 619, 640 (1937), the United States Supreme Court warned that Congress does not possess the right under the Spending Power to demonstrate a "display of arbitrary power." Congressional spending cannot be arbitrary and capricious. The spending power of Congress includes authority to accomplish policy objectives by conditioning receipt of federal funds on compliance with statutory directives, as in the Medicaid program. However, the power is not unlimited and "must be in pursuit of the 'general welfare.' " *South Dakota v. Dole*, 483 U.S. 203, 207 (1987). In *Dole* the Supreme Court stated, "that conditions on federal grants might be illegitimate if they are unrelated to the federal interest in particular national projects or programs." *Id. at 207*. It seems axiomatic that the federal interest in H.R. 3590 is not simply requiring universal health care, but also ensuring that the states share with the federal government the cost of providing such care to their citizens. This federal interest is evident from the fact this legislation would require every state, except Nebraska, to shoulder its fair share of the increased Medicaid costs the bill will generate. The provision of the bill that relieves a single state from this cost-sharing program appears to be not only unrelated, but also antithetical to the legitimate federal interests in the bill.

The fundamental unfairness of H.R. 3590 may also give rise to claims under the due process, equal protection, privileges and immunities clauses and other provisions of the Constitution. As a practical matter, the deal struck by the United States Senate on the "Nebraska Compromise" is a disadvantage to the citizens of 49 states. Every state's tax dollars, except Nebraska's, will be devoted to cost-sharing required by the bill, and will be therefore unavailable for other essential state programs. Only the citizens of Nebraska will be freed from this diminution in state resources for critical state services. Since the only basis for the Nebraska preference is arbitrary and unrelated to the substance of the legislation, it is unlikely that the difference would survive even minimal scrutiny.

We ask that Congress delete the Nebraska provision from the pending legislation, as we prefer to avoid litigation. Because this provision has serious implications for the country and the future of our nation's legislative process, we urge you to take appropriate steps to protect the Constitution and the rights of the citizens of our nation. We believe this issue is readily resolved by removing the provision in question from the bill, and we ask that you do so.

By singling out the particular provision relating to special treatment of Nebraska, we do not suggest there are no other legal or constitutional issues in the proposed health care legislation.

Please let us know if we can be of assistance as you consider this matter.

Sincerely,

Henry McMaster
Attorney General, South Carolina

Rob McKenna
Attorney General, Washington

Mike Cox
Attorney General, Michigan

Greg Abbott
Attorney General, Texas

John Suthers
Attorney General, Colorado

Troy King
Attorney General, Alabama

Wayne Stenehjem
Attorney General, North Dakota

Bill Mims
Attorney General, Virginia

Tom Corbett
Attorney General, Pennsylvania

Mark Shurtleff
Attorney General, Utah

Bill McCollum
Attorney General, Florida

Lawrence Wasden
Attorney General, Idaho

Marty Jackley
Attorney General, South Dakota

Appendix B: Nava-Martinez Order

IN THE UNITED STATES DISTRICT COURT
FOR THE SOUTHERN DISTRICT OF TEXAS
BROWNSVILLE DIVISION

United States District Court
Southern District of Texas
ENTERED

DEC 1 3 2013

David J. Bradley, Clerk of Court

UNITED STATES OF AMERICA,	§	
Plaintiff,	§	
	§	
VS.	§	CRIMINAL NO. B-13-441-1
	§	
	§	
MIRTHA VERONICA NAVA-MARTINEZ,	§	
Defendant.	§	
	§	

ORDER

Mirtha Veronica Nava-Martinez pleaded guilty to attempting to smuggle a ten-year-old El Salvadorean female, Y.P.S., into the United States in violation of 8 U.S.C. § 1324(a)(1)(A)(ii).[1] This Court sentenced Nava-Martinez in accordance with the established federal procedure, the law, and the United States Sentencing Guidelines, and has purposefully waited until after signing that judgment before addressing the issue that is the subject of this Order.

On May 18, 2013, Nava-Martinez, an admitted human trafficker, was caught at the Brownsville & Matamoros Bridge checkpoint. She was trying to smuggle Y.P.S. into the United States using a birth certificate that belonged to one of her daughters. Nava-Martinez had no prior relationship with Y.P.S. and was hired by persons unknown solely to smuggle her into the United States. Nava-Martinez is a resident alien and this was her second felony offense in three years, having committed a food stamp fraud offense in 2011. She was to be paid for smuggling Y.P.S. from Matamoros to Brownsville, although the identity of her immediate payor and the amount are unknown. The details as to how Y.P.S. got to Matamoros, Mexico from El Salvador, and how she

---

[1] The Court will use the minor's initials to protect her identity.

was to get from Brownsville to Virginia were also not disclosed to the Court. This conspiracy was started when Patricia Elizabeth Salmeron Santos solicited human traffickers to smuggle Y.P.S. from El Salvador to Virginia. Salmeron Santos currently lives illegally in the United States. She applied for a tourist visa in 2000, but was turned down. Despite being denied legal entry into the United States, she entered the United States illegally and is living in Virginia.

Salmeron Santos admitted that she started this conspiracy by hiring alien smugglers to transfer her child from El Salvador to Virginia. She agreed to pay $8,500 (and actually paid $6,000 in advance) for these human traffickers to smuggle her daughter. The criminal conspiracy instigated by Salmeron Santos was temporarily interrupted when Nava-Martinez was arrested. Despite this setback, the goal of the conspiracy was successfully completed thanks to the actions of the United States Government. This Court is quite concerned with the apparent policy of the Department of Homeland Security (hereinafter "DHS") of completing the criminal mission of individuals who are violating the border security of the United States. Customs and Border Protection agents stopped the Defendant at the border inspection point. She was arrested, and the child was taken into custody. The DHS officials were notified that Salmeron Santos instigated this illegal conduct. Yet, instead of arresting Salmeron Santos for instigating the conspiracy to violate our border security laws, the DHS delivered the child to her—thus successfully completing the mission of the criminal conspiracy. It did not arrest her. It did not prosecute her. It did not even initiate deportation proceedings for her. This DHS policy is a dangerous course of action.

The DHS, instead of enforcing our border security laws, actually assisted the criminal conspiracy in achieving its illegal goals. The Government's actions were not done in connection with a sting operation or a controlled delivery situation. Rather, the actions it took were directly in furtherance of Y.P.S.'s illegal presence in the United States. It completed the mission of the conspiracy initiated by Salmeron Santos. In summary, instead of enforcing the laws of the United States, the Government took direct steps to help the individuals who violated it. A private citizen would, and should, be prosecuted for this conduct.

This is the fourth case with the same factual situation this Court has had in as many weeks. In all of the cases, human traffickers who smuggled minor children were apprehended short of delivering the children to their ultimate destination. In all cases, a parent, if not both parents, of the children was in this country illegally. That parent initiated the conspiracy to smuggle the minors into the country illegally. He or she also funded the conspiracy. In each case, the DHS completed the criminal conspiracy, instead of enforcing the laws of the United States, by delivering the minors to the custody of the parent illegally living in the United States. In response to this Court's inquiry about this policy in the instant case, the Government responded with a copy of the 1997 *Flores v. Reno*, CV-85-4544-RJK, settlement agreement and a copy of a portion of the Homeland Security Act. No other explanation was offered—no doubt because there is no explanation. The DHS has simply chosen not to enforce the United States' border security laws.

This Court understands that the Government has previously entered into the *Flores* settlement regarding its practices, policies and regulations regarding the treatment and detention of unaccompanied minors. Since that order is apparently sealed, this Court will not quote in detail any specific language. Generally, that settlement requires the Government to release a minor to his or her parent, guardian, or relative, among others, in an order of preference established by the settlement documents. There is nothing in this settlement that prohibits the DHS from arresting Salmeron Santos–the individual who initiated this conspiracy–or from at least initiating deportation proceedings. There was also no explanation of why this settlement agreement—whose terms terminated five years after the date of final court approval—is still even effective. [*Flores Settlement Agreement* ¶ 40].[2] The Government also implies by its response to the Court that the Homeland Security Act of 2002 somehow authorizes its participation in this conspiracy. Again, there is nothing in this Act that directs and authorizes the DHS to turn a blind eye to criminal conduct, and certainly nothing that compels it to participate in and complete the mission of a criminal conspiracy or to encourage parents to put their minor children in perilous situations subject to the whims of evil individuals.[3] These actions are both dangerous and unconscionable.

In each of the four cases, the Government also incurred significant expense to help complete the conspiracy. In all cases when the Government apprehended some of the traffickers, the Government transported the children across the country to unite them with a parent (or parents) who

---

[2] The Government did not provide this Court with the actual, final court order that approved the settlement, so it is unclear when its terms expired.

[3] The only portion of the Act to which the Government cites contains a provision concerning "reuniting unaccompanied alien children with a parent <u>abroad</u> . . . ." 6 U.S.C.A. § 279(b)(1)(H) (West 2013) (emphasis added). More importantly, the relevant section to which this Court has been directed concerns "the care of unaccompanied alien children." *Id.* § 279(a). "Unaccompanied alien child" is a defined term. *Id.* § 279(g)(2). Under the Act, that term refers to a child under the age of eighteen who has no lawful immigration status and with respect to whom:

    (i) There is no parent or legal guardian in the United States; or
    (ii) No parent or legal guardian in the United States is available to provide care and
    physical custody.

Id. § 279(g)(2)(C).
All of the children in question in the cases before this Court were <u>not</u> "unaccompanied alien children" as defined by this Act. All of them had at least one parent in the United States. Furthermore, they evidently all had a parent in the United States available to care for them because the DHS delivered the children to them. Thus the Act cited to this Court has no application and certainly provides no excuse for the Government to continue the criminal activity of the trafficking conspiracy.

4

was in the country illegally. In one situation, the Government flew a child to multiple locations in different parts of the United States. The taxpayers of the United States suffer the expense of delivering these minors. This expense includes not only the cost of paying travel, room and board for the children, but it may also, according to the information supplied to this Court in yet another case, include the salary and travel expenses of a guardian to accompany them. This is an absurd and illogical result. The DHS could reunite the parent and child by apprehending the parent who has committed not one, but at least two different crimes. It would be more efficient for the Government to arrest the individuals who are not only in the country illegally, but while in the country illegally are also fostering illegal conspiracies. It would also be much cheaper to apprehend those co-conspirators and reunite them at the children's location. Yet, it neither prosecutes nor deports the wrongdoer.[4]

The DHS is rewarding criminal conduct instead of enforcing the current laws. More troubling, the DHS is encouraging parents to seriously jeopardize the safety of their children. While Y.P.S. was transported in a car, others are made to swim the Rio Grande River or other bodies of water in remote areas. This concern for the safety of these individuals is not fanciful or theoretical; it is a real and immediate concern. As this Court waited for the judgment to be prepared before it

---

[4]Subsequent to this Court's inquiry into this situation, the United States Attorney's Office has apparently "requested" the DHS place Salmeron Santos in "immigration proceedings." There has been no word as to whether this has been done, but the Government has informed the Court that it will not prosecute these wrongdoers. The Court has not been informed as to the identity of what individual or office initiated this policy, so it must refer to the DHS generically. In another one of the cases, the Government again informed the Court the result would be no prosecutions and only a "request" that immigration proceedings be instigated. There is no indication as to whether this request will be honored. There is not even an indication that the DHS will seek reimbursement of the costs that taxpayers have incurred. That being the case, the DHS should cease telling the citizens of the United States that it is enforcing our border security laws because it is clearly not. Even worse, it is helping those who violate these laws.

released this opinion, two illegal aliens drowned, two more are missing, and a three-year-old El Salvadorean toddler was found abandoned by smugglers—each event occurring just outside of Brownsville.[5]

This Court takes no position on the topic of immigration reform, nor should one read this opinion as a commentary on that issue. That is a subject laced with controversy and is a matter of much political debate which is not the province of the judicial branch. Nevertheless, the failure by the DHS to enforce current United States law concerns this Court for three unassailable reasons.

First, and most importantly, these illegal activities help fund the illegal drug cartels which are a very real danger for both citizens of this country and Mexico.

> Mexican cartels control most of the human smuggling and human trafficking routes and networks in Texas. The nature of the cartels' command and control of human smuggling and human trafficking networks along the border is varied, including cartel members having direct organizational involvement and responsibility over human smuggling and human trafficking operations, as well as cartel members sanctioning and facilitating the operation of human smuggling and human trafficking organizations. In other circumstances, human smuggling organizations are required to pay the cartels for operating their networks and routes in their territory.[6]

This Court need not list the dangers involved for minors, or even adults, who are being smuggled into the United States. In the last year, this Court has seen instances where aliens being smuggled were assaulted, raped, kidnapped and/or killed. This Court's antidotal experiences, however, are not unique.

---

[5]*See, e.g.*, Kayleigh Sommer, *Border Crossing Deaths; One Hospitalized*, BROWNSVILLE HERALD, Dec. 11, 2013, at A2; Marcy Martinez, *Child Smuggled then Abandoned at Laundromat*, Valley Central (Nov. 6, 2013 10:52 PM), http://www.valleycentral.com/news/story.aspx?id=968343#.Uqsq4NJDs3o.

[6]Tex. Dept. of Pub. Safety, Texas Public Safety Threat Overview (2013), at 24–25, http://www.txdps.state.tx.us/director_staff/media_and_communications/threatoverview.pdf.

Mexican cartels, transnational gangs, human trafficking groups, and other criminal organizations engage in a wide range of criminal activity in Texas, including murder, kidnapping, assault, drug trafficking, weapon smuggling, and money laundering. However, by far the most vile crime in which these organizations and other criminals are engaged is the exploitation and trafficking of children. These crimes are also carried out and enabled by prostitution rings, manufacturers and viewers of child pornography, sexual predators, and other criminals. Regardless of who perpetrates these crimes or their motives, this category of criminal activity is especially heinous, as it takes advantage of children and subjects them to violence, extortion, forced labor, sexual assault, or prostitution.

*   *   *   *

The methods and means used by smugglers to transport and hold aliens subject them to high degrees of risk. Unsafe vehicles and drivers, squalid conditions in stash houses, rugged terrain, and harsh elements create dangerous circumstances. Hundreds of illegal aliens have died in Texas and elsewhere along the border. Since FY2008, 2,008 deaths of suspected illegal aliens have been reported along the border, including 839 in Texas sectors. These include deaths due to environmental exposure (heat and cold), terrain and motor-vehicle-related deaths, drownings, other causes, and cases in which skeletal remains were recovered or a cause could not be determined. FY2012 was a record year for such deaths in Texas sectors, increasing 198 percent from 91 in FY2010 to 271 in FY2012. An even greater number of illegal aliens have been rescued from such conditions by law enforcement; since FY2008, 6,375 people have been rescued along the border, including 3,020 in Texas.

In addition to these dangerous methods and means, smugglers also regularly use violence, extortion, and unlawful restraint against illegal aliens. In some cases, they are forced to perform labor, and females—including minors—may be sexually assaulted. Some are subjected to physical assaults if payments are not received, and several have died while being held in stash houses in Texas. And just as drug traffickers may attempt to steal drug loads from rival traffickers, criminals sometimes attempt to steal or hijack groups of aliens from smugglers.[7]

Time and again this Court has been told by representatives of the Government and the defense that cartels control the entire smuggling process. These entities are not known for their concern for human life. They do not hire bonded childcare providers to smuggle children. By fostering an atmosphere whereby illegal aliens are encouraged to pay human smugglers for further

---

[7] *Id.* at 12, 24–25 (emphasis added).

7

services, the Government is not only allowing them to fund the illegal and evil activities of these cartels, but is also inspiring them to do so. The big economic losers in this scenario are the citizens of the United States who, by virtue of this DHS policy, are helping fund these evil ventures with their tax dollars. The overall losers, who endure the consequences of this policy, are the citizens on both sides of the border who suffer from the nefarious activities of the cartels.[8]

Second, the DHS's current policy undermines the deterrent effect the laws may have and inspires others to commit further violations. Those who hear that they should not fear prosecution or deportation will not hesitate, and obviously have not hesitated, to act likewise. They perceive that they have nothing to lose but some time and effort. If the human traffickers are successful, so much the better—mission accomplished. Even if their co-conspirators are unsuccessful, the Government will finish the job of the human traffickers—mission still accomplished. It is no wonder these cases are proliferating. Further, this policy is encouraging individuals to turn their children over to complete strangers—strangers about whom only one thing is truly known: they are criminals involved in a criminal conspiracy.

Children, such as Y.P.S., are especially at risk.

Some children are more vulnerable to exploitation, such as unaccompanied alien children (UAC). Since FY2010, there have been 58,763 UAC apprehensions along the US-Mexico border, including 33,474 in Texas sectors. The number of UAC apprehensions in Texas increased 81 percent from FY2010 to FY2012. UAC apprehensions have also become increasingly concentrated in the state. Texas sectors accounted for 65 percent of all UAC apprehensions along the border in FY2012, up

---

[8]The Court notes parenthetically that it is also common knowledge that these human smugglers will occasionally smuggle methamphetamine, heroin or other illegal and dangerous substances at the same time they smuggle humans. Both Congress and the Fifth Circuit Court of Appeals have recognized, albeit in a different context, that the mixture of children and drug dealers is a grave danger even when no drugs are being distributed. *United States v. Wake*, 948 F.2d 1422, 1433 (5th Cir. 1991).

from 48 percent in FY2010.[9]

An 81% increase in two years should tell the DHS that their policy is failing. If they persist in this policy, more children are going to be harmed, and the DHS will be partly responsible because it encourages this kind of Russian roulette.

Finally, this policy lowers the morale of those law enforcement agents on the front line here on the border. These men and women, with no small risk to their own safety, do their best to enforce our laws and protect the citizens of the United States. It seems shameful that some policymaker in their agency institutes a course of inaction that negates their efforts. It has to be frustrating to those that are actually doing the work of protecting Americans when those efforts are thwarted by a policy that supports the lawbreakers.

This Court is not unsympathetic to any individual or entity taking action that is in the best interests of a minor child; nor is it this Court's goal to divide or separate family members. But the decision to separate Salmeron Santos from Y.P.S. was made years ago, and it was made by Salmeron Santos. She purposefully chose this course of action.[10] Her decision to smuggle the child across the border, even if motivated by the best of motives, is not an excuse for the United States Government to further a criminal conspiracy, and by doing so, encourage others to break the law and endanger

---

[9]*Id.* (emphasis added).

[10]This Court will not address an issue that some may raise: whether it is in the best interests of Y.P.S. to be reunited with a parent who had previously abandoned that child in a different country. Nor will this Court address the issue as to whether a responsible parent would place her child not only in the care of total strangers, but also in the care of total strangers which she knows are criminals. While there could be many reasons, some not without merit, for following such a course, many would certainly argue that most courts in the United States would not find that to be good parenting.

additional children. To put this in another context, the DHS policy is as logical as taking illegal drugs or weapons that it has seized from smugglers and delivering them to the criminals who initially solicited their illegal importation/exportation. Legally, this situation is no different. This Court is not blind to the needs of a minor child, nor is it suggesting that a child should be punished for the crimes of her parent. Nevertheless, neither the *Flores* settlement nor a concern for common decency compels the Government to not only aid, but also reward an individual for initiating a scheme to break the laws governing the border security of this country. Further, neither compels the Government to aid the drug cartels who control this human trafficking.

Finally, the Court is aware that prosecutors and law enforcement officers, including those here on the border, frequently use their discretion to defer the prosecution or arrest of individuals. This Court is not opposed to the concept of prosecutorial discretion, if that discretion is exercised with a sense of justice and common sense. Nevertheless, it is not aware of any accepted legal principle, including prosecutorial discretion, that not only allows the Government to decline prosecution, but further allows it to actually complete the intended criminal mission. The DHS should enforce the laws of the United States—not break them.

Signed this 13th day of December, 2013.

Andrew S. Hanen
United States District Judge

Notes

CHAPTER THREE: UNITY OF FAITH

1 Brief: http://www.americanbar.org/content/dam/aba/publishing/preview/briefs/pdfs/04-05/03_1500Resp.authcheckdam.pdf.
2 Oral argument: https://www.oyez.org/cases/2004/03-1500.
3 http://www.supremecourt.gov/oral_arguments/argument_transcripts/03-1500.pdf.
4 *McCreary County v. American Civil Liberties Union*, 125 S. Ct. 2722 (2005).

CHAPTER FOUR: I THINK WE CAN

1 http://www.politico.com/story/2009/12/payoffs-for-states-get-reid-to-60-030815.
2 http://www.newyorker.com/magazine/2012/06/25/unpopular-mandate.
3 https://www.youtube.com/watch?v=08uk99L8oqQ.
4 http://usatoday30.usatoday.com/news/nation/2010-03-23-attorneys-general-health-suit_N.htm.
5 http://www.wsj.com/articles/SB10001424053111904006104576504383685080762.
6 Ibid.
7 https://www.texasgop.org/ag-greg-abbott-reports-from-the-supreme-court-on-Obamacare/.

CHAPTER FIVE: PRESIDENT OR KING?

1 http://www.galen.org/newsletters/changes-to-obamacare-so-far/.
2 http://www.cnn.com/2013/01/14/politics/schoolhouse-rock-40/.
3 *The Spirit of the Laws*, Book XI, Ch. 6, published 1748.

4 http://swampland.time.com/2012/08/30/what-he-knows-now-obama-on
-popularity-partisanship-and-getting-things-done-in-washington/.

5 Greg Abbott, *Restoring the Rule of Law,* 2016, http://gov.texas.gov/files/press
-office/Restoring_The_Rule_Of_Law_01082016.pdf.

6 http://townhall.com/tipsheet/katiepavlich/2014/11/19/jon-karl-does-obama
-think-hes-emperor-of-the-united-states-n1920606.

7 http://www.factcheck.org/2014/11/obamas-immigration-amnesia/.

8 http://www.cbp.gov/sites/default/files/documents/BP%20Total%20Monthly%20
Apps%20by%20Sector%20and%20Area%2C%20FY2000-FY2015.pdf.

9 http://hotair.com/archives/2014/06/16/young-illegals-tell-border-patrol-were
-coming-because-we-heard-about-a-new-u-s-law-that-lets-minors-stay/.

10 http://www.voanews.com/content/texas-governor-perry-orders-state-national
-guard-to-border/1962520.html.

11 http://thehill.com/news/administration/224955-obama-moves-to-give-legal
-status-to-5-million-illegal-immigrants.

12 https://www.washingtonpost.com/video/politics/obama-i-just-took-action-to
-change-the-law/2016/01/22/62be1cfe-c0df-11e5-98c8-7fab78677d51_video.html.

CHAPTER SIX: POWER AND PROBLEMS

1 http://crimeblog.dallasnews.com/2016/01/reports-iraqi-refugee-arrested-in-
houston-in-alleged-terror-plot.html/.

2 *Federalist* 58.

3 http://www.pewresearch.org/fact-tank/2013/10/09/5-facts-about-the-national
-debt-what-you-should-know/.

4 http://www.mrt.com/business/oil/article_e7f32d45-fab8-5025-afa9
-26a00d768910.html.

5 http://www.acslaw.org/acsblog/ninth-circuit-rejects-commerce-clause-challenge
-to-endangered-species-act-regulation.

6 http://cdn.ca9.uscourts.gov/datastore/opinions/2011/03/25/10-15192.pdf.

7 http://www.eli.org/playing-whack-mole-endangered-species-act.

8 http://www.wsj.com/articles/SB122721278056345271.

9 http://www.crowdfundinsider.com/2016/01/79769-dallas-fed-on-community
-banks-too-small-to-succeed-crushed-by-excessive-regulations/.

CHAPTER EIGHT: THE FIX

1 Helen E. Veit et al., eds., *Creating the Bill of Rights: The Documentary Record from the First Federal Congress* (Baltimore: Johns Hopkins University Press, 1991).

2 Joseph Story, *Commentaries on the Constitution,* Sec. 1822.

3 Veit et al., eds., *Creating the Bill of Rights.*

4 Records of the Federal Convention (reprinted in 4 *Founders' Convention*, 577).

5 Veit et al., eds., *Creating the Bill of Rights*.

6 Russell L. Caplan, *Constitutional Brinkmanship: Amending the Constitution by National Convention* (New York: Oxford University Press, 1988), 73–78, 78–89. Currently there are twenty-seven states with active resolutions calling for a balanced budget amendment, and "[a]s many as 13 more states may take up the matter this year." Editorial, *USA Today*, January 6, 2016, http://www.usatoday.com/story /opinion/2016/01/06/marco-rubio-constitutional-convention-balanced-budget -editorials-debates/78328702/.

7 Cyril F. Brickfield, "Problems Relating to a Federal Constitutional Convention," 85th Congress, 1st Sess., at 8–9, 89 (House Judiciary Committee 1957).

8 Ibid.

9 Ala. H.J.R. 112 (2015); Alaska S.J.R. 18 (2014); Ga. S.R. 736 (2014); Fla. S. Mem. 476, 658 (2014), http://www.tennessean.com/story/news/politics/2016/02/04 /house-approves-call-convention-states/79816402/.

10 http://dispatchesfromcoconutgrove.blogspot.com/2013/06/gregory-watson-in terview.html, https://en.wikipedia.org/wiki/Gregory_Watson, http://writ.news .findlaw.com/dean/20020927.html.

11 Madison Resolution (June 8, 1789), reprinted in Veit et al., eds., *Creating the Bill of Rights*, 14–28.

12 http://m.kiplinger.com/article/investing/T052-C016-S002-how-to-invest-in-a -slowing-u-s-economy.html, http://qz.com/286213/the-chart-obama-haters-love -most-and-the-truth-behind-it/.

CHAPTER NINE: TEETH IN THE TENTH

1 *Garcia v. San Antonio Metropolitan Transit Authority*, 469 U.S. 528 (1985).

2 *New State Ice Co. v. Liebmann*, 285 U.S. 262, 311 (1932) (Brandeis, J., dissenting).

CHAPTER TEN: SECRET AGENCY LAW

1 http://www.forbes.com/sites/waynecrews/2015/07/28/the-problem-with-the -white-house-threat-to-veto-the-reins-act/#83225db4c86e.

2 https://www.washingtonpost.com/opinions/the-rise-of-the-fourth-branch-of -government/2013/05/24/c7faaad0-c2ed-11e2-9fe2-6ee52d0eb7c1_story.html.

3 https://www.usa.gov/federal-agencies/a.

4 https://www.washingtonpost.com/opinions/the-rise-of-the-fourth-branch-of -government/2013/05/24/c7faaad0-c2ed-11e2-9fe2-6ee52d0eb7c1_story.html.

5 https://www.washingtonpost.com/opinions/the-rise-of-the-fourth-branch-of -government/2013/05/24/c7faaad0-c2ed-11e2-9fe2-6ee52d0eb7c1_story.html.

6 John Adams, *Thoughts on Government*, April 1776, reprinted in Philip Kurland,

ed., *The Founders' Constitution*, vol. 1 (Chicago: University of Chicago Press, 1987), 109.

7 John Locke, *Second Treatise of Civil Government* (1690).

8 *Wayman v. Southard*, 23 U.S. 1, 41 (1825).

9 *Marshall Field & Co. v. Clark*, 143 U.S. 649 (1892).

10 See *Panama Refining Co. v. Ryan*, 293 U.S. 388 (1935).

11 See *A.L.A. Schechter Poultry Corp. v. United States*, 295 U.S. 495 (1935).

12 William E. Leuchtenburg, *The Supreme Court Reborn: The Constitutional Revolution in the Age of Roosevelt* (New York: Oxford University Press, 1995) 132–62; Franklin D. Roosevelt, Fireside Chat 9: On "Court-Packing," March 9, 1937, http://millercenter.org/President/speeches/speech-3309.

13 James M. Landis, *The Administrative Process* (New Haven, CT: Yale University Press, 1938), 1.

14 *Federalist* 51, at 322 (Madison), in *The Federalist Papers*, ed. Clinton Rossiter (New York: New American Library, 1961).

15 https://stateimpact.npr.org/texas/2012/04/30/texas-epa-official-resigns-after -crucify-them-controversy/.

16 See Jim Rossi, "Institutional Design and the Lingering Legacy of Antifederalist Separation of Powers Ideals in the States," *Vanderbilt Law Review* 52 (1999): 1167.

17 https://www.whitehouse.gov/the-press-office/2014/05/17/weekly-address -working-when-congress-won-t-act.

CHAPTER ELEVEN: COMMERCE CLAWS

1 http://www.cbsnews.com/news/poll-congress-approval-rating-drops-to-11 -percent/.

2 See Randy E. Barnett, *Restoring the Lost Constitution*, rev ed. (Princeton, NJ: Princeton University Press, 2014), ch. 11.

3 *Gibbons v. Ogden*, 9 Wheat. 1, 194–95 (1824).

4 *A.L.A. Schechter Poultry Corp. v. United States*, 295 U.S. 495 (1935).

5 *United States v. Lopez*, 514 U.S. 549 (1995). See also Leuchtenburg, *The Supreme Court Reborn*, 132–62 (1995); https://en.wikipedia.org/wiki/West_Coast_Hotel _Co._v._Parrish.

6 312 U.S. 100.

7 317 U.S. 111 (1942).

8 http://www.orkin.com/flies/other-types-of-flies/.

9 *National Association of Home Builders v. Babbitt* 130 F.3rd 1041.

10 *National Association of Home Builders v. Babbitt* 130 F.3rd 1041, Sentelle dissenting.

11 *National Association of Home Builders v. Babbitt* 130 F.3rd 1041, Sentelle dissenting;

quoting Judge Alex Kozinski, introduction to *Harvard Journal of Law and Public Policy* 19 (1995).

12　http://www.expressnews.com/news/local/article/Tangled-no-more-highway -project-halted-by-spider-5802782.php.

13　http://tribtalk.org/2015/12/17/the-tangled-web-of-the-commerce-clause/.

CHAPTER TWELVE: OF GROCERIES AND GOVERNMENTS

1　http://classicliberal.tripod.com/jefferson/kercheval.html.

2　http://founders.archives.gov/documents/Jefferson/01-30-02-0398.

3　See *Federalist* 41 (Madison).

4　Annals of Cong., House of Representatives, 1st Cong., 2nd Sess. 1686 (1790).

5　6 Annals of Cong., House of Representatives, 4th Cong., 2nd Sess. 1712 (1796). See David P. Currie, *The Constitution in Congress: The Federalist Period, 1789–1801* (Chicago: University of Chicago Press, 1997), http://press-pubs.uchicago.edu /founders/print_documents/a1_8_1s23.html.

6　http://www.macrotrends.net/1319/dow-jones-100-year-historical-chart.

7　*Steward Machine Co. v. Davis*, 301 U.S. 548 (1937).

8　Ibid., 586–87.

9　*Steward Machine Co. v. Davis*, 301 U.S., at 586–87, where it cites *United States v. Butler*, 287 U.S. 1, 65, 66 for that proposition.

10　Unless otherwise indicated, all data on spending, revenues, debts, and deficits are reported at http://www.usgovernmentspending.com.

11　See http://www.cbpp.org/research/policy-basics-where-do-our-federal-tax -dollars-go.

CHAPTER THIRTEEN: JUDGING JUDGES

1　http://sbmblog.typepad.com/sbm-blog/2011/07/how-many-of-the-founding -fathers-were-lawyers.html.

2　*Federalist* 78 (Hamilton) (capitalization altered).

3　*Federalist* 78, at 464–72 (Hamilton).

4　*See, e.g., Marbury v. Madison*, 5 U.S. (1 Cranch) 137 (1802); *Hayburn's Case*, 2 U.S. (2 Dall.) 409, 410-13 n.(a) (1792) (discussing circuit court opinions by Wilson, Jay, and Iredell).

5　*Federalist* 78.

6　*Restoring the Rule of Law*, Abbott (2016) 37.

7　*Bd. of Cty. Comm'rs, Wabaunsee Cty., Kan. v. Umbehr*, 518 U.S. 668, 711 (1996) (Scalia, J., dissenting).

8　*Restoring the Rule of Law*, Abbott (2016) 46).

9 NEB. CONST. art. V, § 2. and N.D. CONST. art. VI, § 4.

10 Letter from Thomas Jefferson to Abigail Adams (Sept. 11, 1804), reprinted in 8 *The Writings of Thomas Jefferson* 310 (Ford ed. 1897).

CONCLUSION: HOW WE RESPOND TO CHALLENGES

1 Sean Collins Walsh, "Liberal Legal Expert: Don't Dismiss Abbott's Call to Amend the Constitution," *Austin American-Statesman*, January 8, 2016.

2 "A Constitutional Convention: How Well Would It Work?," American Enterprise Institute, May 23, 1979, https://www.aei.org/events/a-constitutional-convention -how-well-would-it-work/.

3 Ibid.

4 Ibid.

Acknowledgments

I am forever grateful to my wife, Cecilia, whose support made the story behind the book possible. I'm also thankful for her patience as I took time away from her to write this.

My daughter, Audrey, has kept me focused on what really matters in life. If parents are truly devoted to raising strong children the world will need far fewer laws.

I would not be governor of Texas, nor would I have even embarked on a path from a hospital bed to the legal battlefield, without the remarkable doctors, nurses, physical therapists, and aides who literally pieced my life back together.

My unfading gratitude goes to my former colleagues at Butler & Binion who showed an unparalleled kindness and goodness. Their uplifting support and generosity fueled my recovery, and still fuel me.

To those who worked with me at the 129th State District Court and at the Texas Supreme Court, I am grateful for all you did to hone my understanding of the law, and its effect on the people of our state.

To the exceptional team I had the privilege to work with at the Office of Attorney General, thank you for your dedicated service to Texans, and for helping me wage battle after battle to protect our citizens and the rule of law. Without you, this would be a very short book.

My family and I want to thank the staff of the governor's office as well as the campaign staff who got me there. Your unyielding commitment to the people of Texas allows me to reap compliments that truly belong to you. It's an honor, and joy, to serve the people of Texas with you.

It is truly treacherous to single out just a few names because so many deserving people go unmentioned. But I think everyone who has worked with me knows that during my years as attorney general and governor, a few people in particular have aided and guided me, and have elevated my constitutional analysis. They include Ted Cruz, Daniel Hodge, Jimmy Blacklock, Reed Clay, and Andy Oldham. All of us have benefited from the aid of Robert Allen, who ensures the trains run on time.

Thanks to my advisor, Dave Carney, who understood the importance of this project and who aided the speed with which it was completed.

Thanks also to Matt Hirsch, who has been my communicator-in-chief the past few years.

Thanks to my writing partners, John Mason and Mike Loomis, who took a crash course in the Constitution, helped me tell my story, and communicate this vision for our country.

To my publisher, Threshold Editions, and my literary agent, Esther Fedorkevich. I appreciate your belief in this book and support of this message of hope for America. Thanks also for helping this project get completed so quickly.

To those who staffed and volunteered in my campaigns, from

state district judge, to Supreme Court, to attorney general, and to Governor, your support inspires me. Every day. Cecilia, Audrey, and I want to thank the citizens of Texas. You are the reason we fight for freedom.

To my God and Savior, for the opportunity, and grace, to respond to my personal challenges, and the challenges our country faces.

To the people of America—those who inspired the Constitution, those who've fought for liberty, those who built the greatest nation in the history of the world—thank you for your commitment to the Constitution. It is needed now more than ever.